THE ULTIMATE

Breville

SMART OVEN AIR FRYER PRO

Cookbook

Unleash Your Inner Chef and Unlock your Oven's full potential with Easy, Healthy & Mouthwatering Recipes for Beginners and Advanced Users

Alex & Jamie
Blake

Legal & Disclaimer

The content of this book is presented for informational, educational, and business purposes only, and is both accurate and truthful to the best of our knowledge.

While every effort has been made to ensure the accuracy of the content, the author cannot be held responsible for any omissions or errors.

Table of Content

Congratulations! You've just unlocked the cheat code to healthy, restaurant-quality meals at home. "The Ultimate Breville Smart Air Fryer Oven Pro Cookbook" isn't just another recipe collection – it's your personal kitchen revolution.

But here's the million-dollar question: **Are YOU ready to become the envy of your dinner parties?** Imagine whipping up crispy, juicy dishes that leave your guests begging for the secret. This book holds that power, with foolproof recipes and expert techniques anyone can master.

Don't let this knowledge gather dust on your shelf. **Turn those "oohs" and "aahs" into a wave of new Breville believers.** Your Amazon review is the key. Share your experience, showcase your culinary triumphs, and inspire others to join the Breville revolution.

Here's your chance to be a hero. Head over to Amazon right now and leave a detailed review. Did this book transform your weeknight meals? Did a specific recipe blow you away? Let the world know!

Feeling like a Breville rockstar? Snap a pic of your latest creation or film a quick video showcasing your skills. Include it with your review and become a legend in the Amazon cookbook community.

Remember, **your review is pure gold**. It helps others unlock the full potential of their Breville and become kitchen superstars themselves. Let's build a Breville army, one rave review at a time!

Unlock Your Breville Bonus Content!
Scan & Supercharge Your Breville Journey

Introduction

Welcome to the world of the Breville Smart Air Fryer Oven Pro, your one-stop shop for delicious and healthy meals! This countertop powerhouse is more than just an air fryer; it's a culinary chameleon with a range of functions that can transform your cooking routine. Forget about single-use appliances cluttering your kitchen. This multitasker can roast a chicken, bake a cake, dehydrate fruit for healthy snacks, and even broil perfectly golden steaks – all within the same sleek unit.

Beyond Air Frying

While the air fryer function is a star attraction, its capabilities extend far beyond crispy French fries. Here's a glimpse into the magic your Breville can create:

- **Roasting**: Imagine juicy, tender turkeys for Thanksgiving or perfectly caramelized vegetables – the Smart Oven Pro's powerful heating elements and convection technology ensure even cooking and exceptional results every time.
- **Baking**: Craving homemade cookies or fluffy cakes? No problem! The baking function provides consistent heat distribution, leading to perfectly golden breads, pastries, and sweet treats.
- **Broiling**: Indulge in restaurant-quality steaks with a beautiful sear or melt cheese on top of your favorite casseroles – the broil function delivers intense heat for a quick browning effect.
- **Dehydrating**: Unlock a world of healthy snacking by dehydrating fruits, vegetables, and even herbs. Preserve the natural flavors of your ingredients and create homemade jerky, fruit leathers, and veggie chips.
- **Pizza Night, Simplified**: Calling all pizza lovers! The "Pizza" function preheats your oven to the ideal temperature, ensuring a crispy crust and perfectly melted cheese. Ditch the lengthy preheating times of your conventional oven and enjoy restaurant-style pizza in a fraction of the time with the Breville Smart Air Fryer Oven Pro.
- **Proofing Perfection**: Aspiring bakers, rejoice! The "Proof" function provides the perfect warm, humid environment for your yeast to rise. Imagine perfectly risen bread dough or fluffy pizza dough, all thanks to the controlled heat and moisture of this specialized setting.
- **Reheat Like a Pro**: Say goodbye to soggy leftovers with the "Reheat" function. This setting gently reheats food, ensuring even warming without drying out your leftovers. From pizza slices to casseroles, the "Reheat" function revives your favorite dishes to a delicious, just-cooked state.
- **The Perfect Batch, Every Time**: Indulge your sweet tooth with the "Cookies" function. This pre-programmed setting delivers the ideal temperature and cooking time for perfectly baked cookies, every single time. No more experimentation with temperatures or undercooked centers – the "Cookies" function guarantees consistent, delightful results.

- **Slow Cooker Magic**: Transform tough cuts of meat into melt-in-your-mouth masterpieces with the "Slow Cook" function. This setting allows you to cook low and slow, drawing out the flavors and creating incredibly tender and flavorful dishes. Perfect for weeknight dinners or weekend slow-cooked delights, this function offers a convenient and hands-off approach to home cooking.
- **Bagel Bliss**: Achieve that perfect toasted exterior with a chewy, soft center for your bagels with the dedicated "Bagel" function. This setting offers precise heat distribution to ensure even browning on both sides, resulting in the ideal bagel experience every time.
- **Toast Your Way**: Start your day right with perfectly toasted bread. The "Toast" function allows you to customize the browning level to your preference, ensuring consistently crisp toast without any burnt edges.

Revolutionize Your Cooking

The Breville Smart Air Fryer Oven Pro isn't just about versatility; it's about making your life easier and healthier. Here's how:

- **Effortless Cooking**: Say goodbye to preheating multiple appliances or hovering over the stove. The Breville offers pre-programmed settings for many functions, allowing you to simply set it and forget it.
- **Farewell to Frying Woes**: Craving crispy fried chicken without the guilt? Air frying uses significantly less oil than traditional methods, resulting in healthier and lighter versions of your favorite fried foods.
- **Faster Than Your Average Oven**: The convection technology in the Breville circulates hot air efficiently, leading to faster cooking times compared to conventional ovens. This translates to less time spent in the kitchen and more time to enjoy your delicious meals.
- **Space-Saving Efficiency**: Consolidate your countertop appliances with this multifunctional wonder. The Breville Smart Air Fryer Oven Pro eliminates the need for separate air fryers, dehydrators, toasters, and even toaster ovens, freeing up valuable counter space.

This is just the beginning of your exciting culinary journey with the Breville Smart Air Fryer Oven Pro. As you delve deeper into this user-friendly appliance, you'll discover a world of possibilities and unlock a whole new level of convenience and healthy cooking in your kitchen. Let's get started on making some delicious magic!

Mastering Your Breville Smart Air Fryer Oven Pro: Tips and Tricks for Kitchen Triumphs

Congratulations on owning the Breville Smart Air Fryer Oven Pro! Now, let's unlock its full potential and transform you into a countertop culinary master. Here are some essential techniques to ensure crispy textures, juicy meats, and perfectly baked goods in every dish

Crispy Perfection

- **The Power of Preheat**: Just like a conventional oven, preheating is crucial for achieving crispy results, especially with air frying. Preheating allows the cooking surface to reach optimal temperature, ensuring your food sears quickly and locks in moisture for a juicy interior.
- **Don't Crowd the Basket**: Overcrowding restricts airflow, leading to soggy, steamed food instead of crispy perfection. Arrange food in a single layer with space between pieces for optimal air circulation.
- **Embrace the Mist**: A light coating of oil helps achieve a crispy exterior, especially with breaded or frozen foods. Use a mister to apply a thin layer of oil instead of drizzling, which can lead to pooling and uneven cooking.

Juicy Meats

- **Pat it Dry**: Excess moisture on the surface of meat prevents proper browning. Pat your meat dry with paper towels before air frying to ensure a beautiful sear and juicy interior.
- **Marinating Magic**: Marinate your meats before air frying for added flavor and tenderness. The Breville's pre-programmed settings allow for easy marinating and air frying in one appliance.
- **The Flip Side**: For thicker cuts of meat like chicken breasts or pork chops, flipping them halfway through cooking ensures even browning and prevents drying out.

Baking Brilliance

- **Lining Up Success**: For baked goods like cookies or pastries, using parchment paper liners prevents sticking and makes cleanup a breeze. The Breville comes with baking trays specifically designed for use with parchment paper.
- **Filling Up Wisely**: Don't overfill baking pans when using the baking function. This can lead to uneven baking and undercooked centers. Refer to your recipe or the Breville's user manual for recommended filling quantities.

- **Mastering the Rack**: Utilizing the different rack positions within the Breville can significantly impact baking results. For even browning on top and bottom, use the middle rack for most baking tasks.

Stacking Smartly (Optional Feature)

If your Breville model features a stacking function, here are some tips for maximizing its potential:
- **Light on Top, Heavy on Bottom**: Place lighter, more delicate items like vegetables or fish on the top rack for faster cooking. Reserve the bottom rack for heavier or denser foods like meats and potatoes that require longer cook times.
- **Double the Fun**: Use the stacking feature to cook multiple dishes simultaneously, saving time and effort. For example, roast vegetables on the top rack while baking salmon on the bottom rack for a complete meal in one go.

Accessorize for Success

Breville offers a variety of accessories specifically designed to enhance your air-frying experience. Here are some popular options and how to use them:

- **Crisp Trays**: These elevated trays allow for better airflow around food, promoting crispier textures, especially for fatty meats or foods with drippings.
- **Rotisserie Basket**: Roast a whole chicken to juicy perfection with the rotisserie basket. The rotating feature ensures even cooking throughout.
- **Skewers**: Utilize skewers with the air frying function to create kabobs with vegetables, meats, or seafood for a fun and flavorful meal option.

By incorporating these tips and tricks, you'll be well on your way to mastering your Breville Smart Air Fryer Oven Pro. Experiment with different techniques, explore the variety of functions, and get ready to create delicious and healthy meals with ease in your very own kitchen!

Reap the Rewards: Health Benefits of Air Frying with Your Breville Smart Air Fryer Oven Pro

Let's face it, we all crave the crispy, golden perfection of fried foods. But traditional deep-frying often comes packed with unhealthy consequences: excess fat, added calories, and potential carcinogens from overheated oil. Thankfully, the Breville Smart Air Fryer Oven Pro offers a revolutionary solution – delicious fried flavors without the guilt! Here's how air frying with your Breville benefits your health:

Fat Fighter

- **Ditch the Deep Fryer**: Deep frying involves submerging food in hot oil, leading to significant fat absorption. Air frying, on the other hand, uses minimal oil, often just a single tablespoon, to achieve a crispy texture. This translates to a dramatic reduction in overall fat content compared to deep-fried foods.
- **Unlock the Power of Air**: The Breville utilizes rapid air circulation to cook food, creating a crispy exterior similar to deep frying. This eliminates the need for excessive oil, making air-fried options significantly lower in fat.

Calorie Conqueror

- **Slash the Calories**: Since air frying uses minimal oil, it naturally reduces the calorie content of your favorite dishes. This makes air frying a perfect choice for those watching their weight or following a calorie-conscious diet.
- **Embrace Healthier Alternatives**: With the Breville, you can enjoy air-fried versions of classically high-calorie foods like French fries, chicken wings, and onion rings. This allows you to indulge in your cravings without sabotaging your health goals.

A Healthier Way to Cook

- **Reduced Harmful Compounds**: Deep frying oil reaches high temperatures, which can lead to the formation of acrylamide, a potentially harmful compound linked to certain health risks. Air frying cooks at lower temperatures, minimizing the formation of acrylamide and promoting a healthier cooking method.
- **Preserving Nutrients**: Air frying cooks food quickly, helping to retain more vitamins and minerals compared to traditional frying methods. This ensures you're getting the most nutritional value out of your ingredients.
- **Heart-Healthy Helper**: By reducing fat and calories, air frying contributes to a heart-healthy lifestyle. With the Breville, you can enjoy delicious meals without worrying about the negative effects of deep-fried foods on your cardiovascular health.

The Breville Smart Air Fryer Oven Pro goes beyond just convenience; it's a game-changer for health-conscious cooks. By embracing air frying, you can create delicious meals that are lower in fat, calories, and potentially harmful compounds. So ditch the deep fryer, embrace the air fryer revolution, and unlock a world of healthy and flavorful possibilities with your Breville!

BREAKFAST DELIGHTS
QUICK AND SATISFYING
STARTS WITH YOUR BREVILLE

Kickstart your day with a delicious and healthy breakfast using the versatile functions of your Breville Smart Air Fryer Oven Pro! This chapter offers ten quick and satisfying recipes to fuel your mornings and keep you energized throughout the day.

Alex & Jamie
Blake

SERVES	PREP TIME	COOK TIME
4	10 minutes	10 minutes

AIR-FRIED BREAKFAST BURRITOS

Ingredients

- 4 large eggs
- 1 tablespoon olive oil
- ¼ cup chopped onion
- ½ red bell pepper, diced
- ¼ cup chopped chorizo (or cooked breakfast sausage)
- ½ cup shredded cheddar cheese
- 4 large flour tortillas
- Salt and pepper to taste
- Optional toppings: Salsa, sour cream, hot sauce, avocado slices

Instructions

1. Preheat your Breville Smart Air Fryer Oven Pro to 400°F (200°C).
2. In a large skillet, heat olive oil over medium heat. Add the chopped onion and bell pepper, and cook until softened, about 5 minutes.
3. Crumble the chorizo (or sausage) into the pan and cook until browned, breaking it up with a spoon.
4. In a separate bowl, whisk the eggs with a pinch of salt and pepper.
5. Pour the whisked eggs into the pan with the cooked vegetables and chorizo. Scramble the eggs until just set.
6. Remove the pan from heat and stir in the shredded cheese.
7. Lay out the flour tortillas on a flat surface. Divide the scrambled egg mixture evenly among the tortillas.
8. Fold the bottom of the tortilla up over the filling, then fold in the sides. Roll the tortilla tightly to form a burrito.
9. Lightly spray the air fryer basket with cooking spray. Place the burritos seam-side down in the basket, ensuring they don't touch.
10. Air fry for 5-7 minutes, or until golden brown and crispy.
11. Serve hot with your favorite toppings like salsa, sour cream, hot sauce, and avocado slices.

Tips

- Feel free to customize your breakfast burritos with your favorite fillings. Chopped mushrooms, black beans, or scrambled tofu are great alternatives.
- You can prepare the scrambled egg mixture and filling ahead of time and assemble the burritos right before air frying for a quick and easy breakfast option.

Nutritional Information (per serving)

Calories: 350, **Fat**: 18g,
Protein: 15g, **Carbs**: 25g

Wrap up a fiesta in a tortilla! These air-fried breakfast burritos are perfect for a grab-and-go breakfast or a satisfying weekend brunch.

7

FLUFFY AIR FRYER PANCAKES

Ingredients

- 1 ½ cups all-purpose flour
- 2 tablespoons sugar
- 2 teaspoons baking powder
- ½ teaspoon salt
- 1 ¼ cups milk
- 1 egg
- 2 tablespoons melted butter

Instructions

1. Preheat your Breville Smart Air Fryer Oven Pro to 350°F (175°C) using the bake function.
2. In a large bowl, whisk together the flour, sugar, baking powder, and salt.
3. In a separate bowl, whisk together the milk, egg, and melted butter.
4. Pour the wet ingredients into the dry ingredients and whisk until just combined. Be careful not to overmix. A few small lumps are okay.
5. Lightly grease a baking sheet or use parchment paper liners.
6. Pour ¼ cup portions of batter onto the baking sheet, leaving space between each pancake for spreading.
7. Air fry for 4-5 minutes per side, or until golden brown and cooked through. You can peek halfway through and gently flip the pancakes using a spatula.
8. Serve hot with your favorite toppings like maple syrup, fresh fruit, whipped cream, or chocolate chips.

Tips

- For thicker pancakes, use ½ cup batter per pancake and air fry for an additional minute per side.
- Add a splash of vanilla extract to the batter for extra flavor.
- You can use buttermilk instead of milk for even fluffier pancakes.

Nutritional Information
(per serving)
Calories: 300, **Fat**: 12g,
Protein: 6g, **Carbs**: 40g

Indulge in classic pancakes without the stovetop splatter! These fluffy air-fried pancakes are perfect for a delicious and mess-free breakfast.

SERVES
4

PREP TIME
10 minutes

COOK TIME
15 - 20 minutes

SAVORY EGG MUFFINS

Ingredients

- 6 large eggs
- ¼ cup chopped onion
- ½ cup chopped bell pepper (any color)
- ½ cup chopped spinach or kale
- ½ cup crumbled feta cheese
- ¼ cup shredded cheddar cheese
- Salt and pepper to taste
- Optional additions: Chopped cooked ham, crumbled sausage, diced mushrooms

Instructions

1. Preheat your Breville Smart Air Fryer Oven Pro to 350°F (175°C). Grease a muffin tin with cooking spray or use paper muffin liners.
2. In a large bowl, whisk together the eggs with a pinch of salt and pepper.
3. Sauté the chopped onion and bell pepper in a skillet with a little olive oil over medium heat until softened, about 5 minutes. Add any other desired cooked vegetables like chopped ham or sausage at this point.
4. Stir the cooked vegetables and the chopped spinach or kale into the whisked eggs.
5. Divide the egg mixture evenly among the prepared muffin cups.
6. Sprinkle the tops of each muffin with crumbled feta cheese and shredded cheddar cheese.
7. Air fry for 15-20 minutes, or until the egg muffins are set and cooked through. You can insert a toothpick into the center of a muffin; it should come out clean when the muffins are done.
8. Let the egg muffins cool slightly before removing them from the muffin tin. Serve warm or at room temperature.

Tips

- Feel free to experiment with different vegetables and cheese combinations. Chopped broccoli, mushrooms, or sun-dried tomatoes are great options.
- You can prepare a large batch of egg muffins on the weekend and store them in the refrigerator for a quick and easy breakfast option throughout the week.

Nutritional Information
(per serving)
Calories: 150, **Fat**: 9g,
Protein: 12g, **Carbs**: 2g

Prepare a batch of mini egg frittatas for a grab-and-go breakfast.

SERVES
4

PREP TIME
10 minutes

COOK TIME
20 - 25 minutes

HEALTHY OATMEAL BAKES

Ingredients

- 1 cup rolled oats
- 1 cup milk (dairy or non-dairy)
- ½ cup plain yogurt (Greek yogurt preferred)
- ½ cup chopped fresh fruit (berries, apples, bananas)
- ¼ cup chopped nuts (walnuts, almonds, pecans)
- 1 tablespoon honey
- 1 teaspoon ground cinnamon
- ¼ teaspoon salt

Instructions

1. Preheat your Breville Smart Air Fryer Oven Pro to 375°F (190°C) using the bake function.
2. In a large bowl, combine the rolled oats, milk, yogurt, chopped fruit, chopped nuts, honey, cinnamon, and salt. Stir well to combine all ingredients.
3. Divide the oatmeal mixture evenly among four ramekins or small baking dishes.
4. Air fry for 20-25 minutes, or until the oatmeal bakes are set and the tops are golden brown.
5. Let the oatmeal bakes cool slightly before serving. You can enjoy them warm or at room temperature.

Tips

- Feel free to substitute different fruits and nuts based on your preference. Dried fruits like raisins or cranberries can also be used.
- For a richer flavor, drizzle a teaspoon of melted butter or coconut oil over the oatmeal mixture before air frying.
- You can top your oatmeal bakes with a dollop of yogurt, a drizzle of honey, or a sprinkle of chia seeds for extra flavor and nutrition.

Alex & Jamie Blake

Nutritional Information
(per serving)
Calories: 300, **Fat**: 6g,
Protein: 10g, **Carbs**: 45g

Transform your oatmeal routine with a delicious baked version. These healthy oatmeal bakes are packed with fiber, protein, and fruit.

SERVES	PREP TIME	COOK TIME
2	5 minutes	5 - 7 minutes

AIR-FRIED BREAKFAST QUESADILLAS

Ingredients

- 2 large flour tortillas
- 2 large eggs, scrambled
- ¼ cup black beans, drained and rinsed
- ½ cup shredded cheddar cheese
- ¼ cup chopped tomato
- ¼ cup chopped avocado
- Salt and pepper to taste
- Chopped fresh cilantro (optional)
- Salsa or hot sauce for serving

Instructions

1. Preheat your Breville Smart Air Fryer Oven Pro to 350°F (175°C).
2. In a small skillet, scramble the eggs with a pinch of salt and pepper.
3. Lay out a flour tortilla on a flat surface. Spread half of the scrambled eggs evenly over one half of the tortilla.
4. Sprinkle half of the shredded cheese, black beans, chopped tomato, and chopped avocado over the scrambled eggs.
5. Fold the tortilla in half, enclosing the filling.
6. Lightly spray the air fryer basket with cooking spray. Place the quesadilla seam-side down in the basket.
7. Air fry for 3-4 minutes per side, or until golden brown and crispy.
8. Repeat steps 3-7 to prepare the second quesadilla.
9. Serve hot with your favorite toppings like salsa, hot sauce, and chopped fresh cilantro (optional).

Tips

- Feel free to customize your breakfast quesadillas with your favorite fillings. Chopped chorizo (or cooked breakfast sausage), diced bell peppers, or crumbled queso fresco are great alternatives.
- You can prepare the scrambled eggs and fillings ahead of time and assemble the quesadillas right before air frying for a quick and easy breakfast option.
- Brush the tortillas with a little melted butter before assembling the quesadillas for extra flavor and crispiness.

Nutritional Information (per serving)

Calories: 400, **Fat**: 18g,
Protein: 15g, **Carbs**: 35g

Elevate your morning routine with cheesy quesadillas. These air-fried breakfast quesadillas are a quick and delicious way to start your day.

| SERVES 4 | PREP TIME 10 minutes | COOK TIME 15 - 20 minutes |

AIR-FRIED BREAKFAST HASH BROWNS

Ingredients

- 2 large russet potatoes, peeled and grated
- 1 small onion, diced
- 1 tablespoon olive oil
- ½ teaspoon salt
- ¼ teaspoon black pepper

Instructions

1. Preheat your Breville Smart Air Fryer Oven Pro to 400°F (200°C).
2. Grate the potatoes using the coarse side of a box grater.
3. Place the grated potatoes in a colander and rinse them under cold water until the water runs clear. This removes excess starch, helping to achieve crispy hash browns.
4. Squeeze out as much moisture as possible from the grated potatoes using a clean kitchen towel or cheesecloth.
5. In a large bowl, combine the grated potatoes, diced onion, olive oil, salt, and pepper. Mix well to coat the potatoes evenly.
6. Form the potato mixture into small patties (about ⅓ cup each).
7. Lightly spray the air fryer basket with cooking spray. Arrange the hash brown patties in a single layer, ensuring they don't touch.
8. Air fry for 15-20 minutes, or until golden brown and crispy on the outside and tender on the inside. You may need to flip the hash brown patties halfway through cooking for even browning.
9. Serve hot with your favorite breakfast toppings like ketchup, sour cream, or hot sauce.

Tips

- For extra crispy hash browns, preheat the air fryer basket for a few minutes before adding the potato patties.
- Feel free to add your favorite seasonings to the hash browns like garlic powder, paprika, or cayenne pepper for a flavor boost.
- You can shred the potatoes ahead of time and store them in a bowl of cold water to prevent browning. Just be sure to rinse them well before forming the patties.

Nutritional Information (per serving)

Calories: 150, **Fat**: 5g,
Protein: 2g, **Carbs**: 25g

Ditch the greasy hash browns! These air-fried breakfast hash browns are a healthier and more flavorful alternative.

SERVES
1

PREP TIME
5 minutes

COOK TIME
15 - 20 minutes

AIR-FRIED SWEET POTATO TOAST

Ingredients

- 1 large sweet potato, sliced into ½ inch thick rounds
- 1 tablespoon olive oil
- ¼ teaspoon salt
- ¼ teaspoon black pepper
- ¼ cup mashed avocado
- 1 fried egg
- Everything bagel seasoning (optional)

Instructions

1. Preheat your Breville Smart Air Fryer Oven Pro to 400°F (200°C).
2. Slice the sweet potato into ½ inch thick rounds.
3. In a large bowl, toss the sweet potato slices with olive oil, salt, and pepper. Ensure all slices are evenly coated.
4. Arrange the sweet potato slices in a single layer on the air fryer basket.
5. Air fry for 15-20 minutes, or until the sweet potato slices are tender and slightly golden brown. You may need to flip the slices halfway through cooking for even browning.
6. While the sweet potato toasts are air frying, prepare your fried egg. Heat a small amount of oil in a skillet over medium heat. Crack an egg into the skillet and cook until the whites are set and the yolk is cooked to your preference.
7. Once the sweet potato toasts are cooked, remove them from the air fryer basket and spread a layer of mashed avocado on each slice.
8. Top with the fried egg.
9. Sprinkle with everything bagel seasoning (optional) for added flavor and texture.
10. Serve hot and enjoy!

Tips

- You can preheat your skillet while the sweet potato toasts are air frying to save time.
- Feel free to experiment with different toppings for your sweet potato toast. Chopped vegetables, crumbled feta cheese, or a drizzle of hot sauce are great options.
- If you prefer a softer texture for your sweet potato toast, microwave the slices for a minute or two before air frying.

Nutritional Information (per serving)

Calories: 350, **Fat**: 15g, **Protein**: 10g, **Carbs**: 40g

Embrace a trendy breakfast option with a twist! Sweet potato toast is a delicious and nutritious alternative to traditional toast.

AIR-FRIED YOGURT PARFAITS WITH GRANOLA

Ingredients

- 1 cup plain Greek yogurt
- ½ cup granola
- ½ cup chopped fresh fruit (berries, banana, mango)
- 1 tablespoon honey (optional)

Instructions

1. Preheat your Breville Smart Air Fryer Oven Pro to 350°F (175°C).
2. Spread the granola evenly on a baking sheet or use parchment paper liners.
3. Air fry the granola for 5-7 minutes, or until golden brown and fragrant. Stir the granola occasionally to ensure even browning.
4. In a serving glass or bowl, layer the Greek yogurt, chopped fruit, and air-fried granola.
5. Drizzle with honey (optional) for extra sweetness.
6. Serve immediately and enjoy!

Tips

- You can use pre-made granola for this recipe. However, air-frying your own granola allows you to control the sweetness and customize it with your favorite nuts, seeds, and dried fruits.
- Feel free to experiment with different yogurt flavors and fruits for variety.
- You can prepare the yogurt parfaits ahead of time and store them in the refrigerator for a grab-and-go breakfast option. Simply assemble the layers in the serving glasses and top with the air-fried granola just before serving.

Alex & Jamie Blake

Nutritional Information
(per serving)
Calories: 300, **Fat**: 8g,
Protein: 15g, **Carbs**: 35g

Layer yogurt, granola, and your favorite fruits for a quick and refreshing breakfast. Air-fried granola adds a delightful crunchy topping.

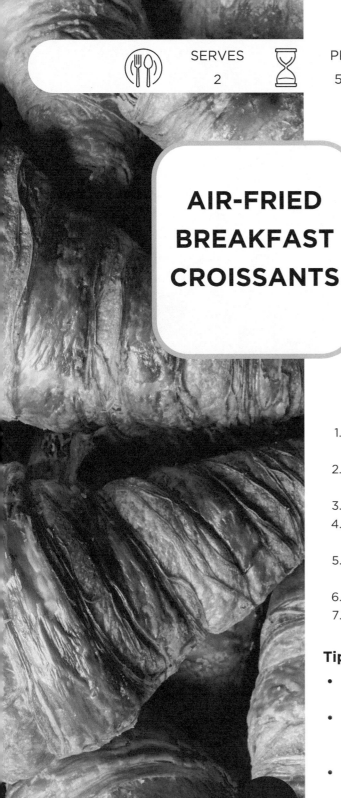

| SERVES 2 | PREP TIME 5 minutes | COOK TIME 5 - 7 minutes |

AIR-FRIED BREAKFAST CROISSANTS

Ingredients

- 2 large croissants
- 1 tablespoon melted butter
- 2 tablespoons granulated sugar
- ¼ teaspoon ground cinnamon

Instructions

1. Preheat your Breville Smart Air Fryer Oven Pro to 375°F (190°C).
2. Brush the melted butter over the top and sides of the croissants.
3. In a small bowl, combine the granulated sugar and cinnamon.
4. Sprinkle the cinnamon sugar mixture evenly over the buttered croissants.
5. Place the croissants in the air fryer basket, ensuring they don't touch.
6. Air fry for 5-7 minutes, or until golden brown and flaky.
7. Serve hot immediately. You can enjoy them plain or with your favorite toppings like jam, honey, or whipped cream.

Tips

- For an extra decadent treat, fill the croissants with a dollop of whipped cream or Nutella before air frying.
- If your croissants are frozen, thaw them completely before air frying. Frozen croissants may require a few extra minutes of cooking time.
- You can use a pastry brush to apply the melted butter and cinnamon sugar mixture for more even coverage.

Nutritional Information (per serving)
Calories: 400, **Fat**: 20g,
Protein: 5g, **Carbs**: 45g

Transform store-bought croissants into a decadent breakfast treat. These air-fried croissants are a quick and easy way to enjoy a flaky and buttery pastry.

SERVES	PREP TIME	COOK TIME
4	10 minutes	20 - 25 minutes

AIR-FRIED BREAKFAST FRITTATA

Ingredients

- 8 large eggs
- ¼ cup chopped onion
- ½ red bell pepper, diced
- ½ cup chopped mushrooms
- ½ cup shredded mozzarella cheese
- ¼ cup crumbled feta cheese
- Salt and pepper to taste
- Optional additions: Chopped cooked ham, chopped spinach or kale, diced tomatoes

Instructions

1. Preheat your Breville Smart Air Fryer Oven Pro to 350°F (175°C) using the bake function. Grease an oven-safe pie dish or small baking pan with cooking spray.
2. In a large skillet, heat a tablespoon of olive oil over medium heat. Sauté the chopped onion, bell pepper, and mushrooms until softened, about 5 minutes.
3. Whisk the eggs together with a pinch of salt and pepper.
4. Stir the cooked vegetables and any additional desired ingredients (cooked ham, spinach, tomatoes) into the whisked eggs.
5. Pour the egg mixture into the prepared baking dish.
6. Sprinkle the top of the frittata with shredded mozzarella cheese and crumbled feta cheese.
7. Air fry for 20-25 minutes, or until the frittata is set and golden brown on top. You can insert a toothpick into the center of the frittata; it should come out clean when the frittata is done.
8. Let the frittata cool slightly before slicing and serving.

Tips

- Feel free to experiment with different vegetables and cheeses in your frittata. Chopped broccoli, asparagus, or sun-dried tomatoes are great options.
- You can prepare the frittata mixture ahead of time and store it in the refrigerator overnight. Simply assemble the frittata in the baking dish and air fry it in the morning for a quick and easy breakfast.
- Serve the air-fried breakfast frittata with a side of toast or fresh fruit for a complete and satisfying breakfast.

Nutritional Information (per serving)

Calories: 300, **Fat**: 15g,
Protein: 20g, **Carbs**: 5g

Whip up a classic frittata in your Breville. This air-fried version is lighter and healthier than traditional stovetop frittatas.

SNACK ATTACK
10 CROWD-PLEASING FINGER FOODS

Fire up your Breville Smart Air Fryer Oven Pro and prepare to satisfy your cravings with these delicious and fun finger foods! Perfect for game nights, movie marathons, after-school treats, or whenever you need a satisfying bite, this collection offers a variety of options to please any palate.

Alex & Jamie
Blake

SERVES	PREP TIME	COOK TIME
4	15 minutes	8 - 10 minutes

AIR-FRIED MOZZARELLA STICKS

Ingredients

- 4 ounces low-moisture mozzarella cheese, cut into sticks
- ½ cup all-purpose flour
- 2 large eggs, beaten
- 1 cup panko breadcrumbs
- ¼ teaspoon paprika
- ¼ teaspoon garlic powder
- Salt and pepper to taste
- Cooking spray

Instructions

1. Preheat your Breville Smart Air Fryer Oven Pro to 400°F (200°C). Lightly grease the air fryer basket with cooking spray.
2. In a shallow bowl, place the flour. In another shallow bowl, whisk the eggs. In a third shallow bowl, combine the panko breadcrumbs, paprika, and garlic powder. Season with salt and pepper to taste.
3. Dredge each mozzarella stick in the flour, coating it evenly. Dip it next in the beaten eggs, ensuring complete coverage. Finally, roll the mozzarella stick in the panko breadcrumb mixture, pressing gently to adhere the crumbs.
4. Place the breaded mozzarella sticks in a single layer in the air fryer basket, ensuring they don't touch. You may need to cook them in batches depending on the size of your air fryer basket.
5. Air fry for 8-10 minutes, or until golden brown and crispy on the outside, and the cheese is melted and gooey on the inside.
6. Serve hot with your favorite dipping sauce like marinara sauce, ranch dressing, or honey mustard.

Tips

- Freeze the breaded mozzarella sticks for at least 30 minutes before air frying for an extra crispy exterior and to prevent the cheese from leaking out during cooking.
- You can use shredded mozzarella cheese instead of sticks, forming them into small balls before breading and air frying.
- Feel free to substitute panko breadcrumbs with crushed crackers or cornflakes for a different flavor and texture.

Alex & Jamie
Blake

Nutritional Information (per serving)

Calories: 350, **Fat**: 18g, **Protein**: 15g, **Carbs**: 25g

These melty cheese sticks are a classic party favorite, and the air fryer makes them healthier and less greasy than deep-frying.

18

|  | SERVES 4 | PREP TIME 15 minutes | COOK TIME 25 - 30 minutes |

CRISPY AIR-FRIED CHICKEN WINGS

Ingredients

- 1 pound chicken wings, separated at the joint (drumettes and wingettes)
- 1 tablespoon olive oil
- 1 teaspoon paprika
- ½ teaspoon garlic powder
- ½ teaspoon onion powder
- ¼ teaspoon cayenne pepper (optional)
- Salt and pepper to taste
- Your favorite wing sauce (optional)

Instructions

1. Preheat your Breville Smart Air Fryer Oven Pro to 400°F (200°C). Pat the chicken wings dry with paper towels to remove any surface moisture.
2. In a large bowl, toss the chicken wings with olive oil, paprika, garlic powder, onion powder, cayenne pepper (if using), salt, and pepper. Ensure all wings are evenly coated with the spice mixture.
3. Arrange the chicken wings in a single layer in the air fryer basket, ensuring they don't touch. You may need to cook them in batches depending on the size of your air fryer basket.
4. Air fry for 20-25 minutes, or until the chicken wings are cooked through and the internal temperature reaches 165°F (74°C). During cooking, flip the wings halfway through for even browning.
5. In the last 5 minutes of cooking, you can brush the wings with your favorite wing sauce for an extra layer of flavor. Be sure to choose a sauce suitable for air frying.
6. Serve hot with your favorite dipping sauces like ranch dressing, blue cheese dressing, or celery sticks and carrots.

Tips

- To remove even more fat from the chicken wings, pat them dry with paper towels after air frying for a few minutes.
- For extra crispy skin, preheat the air fryer for a few minutes before adding the chicken wings.
- Marinate the chicken wings for at least 30 minutes in your favorite marinade for added flavor.

Nutritional Information (per serving)

Calories: 400, **Fat**: 30g, **Protein**: 30g, **Carbs**: 5g

These flavorful chicken wings are a game-day staple! The air fryer ensures crispy skin without the mess of deep-frying.

Alex & Jamie Blake

ROASTED CHICKPEAS

Ingredients

- 1 (15 oz) can chickpeas, drained and rinsed
- 1 tablespoon olive oil
- ½ teaspoon ground cumin
- ¼ teaspoon paprika
- ¼ teaspoon garlic powder
- Salt and pepper to taste

Instructions

1. Preheat your Breville Smart Air Fryer Oven Pro to 400°F (200°C).
2. Pat the drained chickpeas dry with a paper towel to remove any excess moisture. This is crucial for achieving crispy chickpeas.
3. In a large bowl, toss the chickpeas with olive oil, cumin, paprika, garlic powder, salt, and pepper. Ensure all chickpeas are evenly coated with the spice mixture.
4. Spread the chickpeas in a single layer on the air fryer basket, ensuring they don't touch.
5. Air fry for 25-30 minutes, or until golden brown and crispy. Shake the basket occasionally for even browning.
6. Let the roasted chickpeas cool slightly before serving. Enjoy them plain or sprinkle with additional spices like chili powder or cayenne pepper for a kick.

Tips

- Experiment with different spices and herbs to create your own flavor variations. Try dried oregano, rosemary, or a sprinkle of Everything Bagel Seasoning.
- Roast the chickpeas for an additional 5 minutes if you prefer them extra crispy.
- Roasted chickpeas can be stored in an airtight container at room temperature for up to a week.

Nutritional Information (per serving)

Calories: 150, **Fat**: 5g,
Protein: 6g, **Carbs**: 20g

These crunchy and protein-packed roasted chickpeas are a healthy and addictive snack option.

SERVES	PREP TIME	COOK TIME
4	15 minutes	20 - 25 minutes

VEGGIE FRIES WITH HOMEMADE KETCHUP

Ingredients

For the Veggie Fries:
- 2 large potatoes, cut into thin sticks
- 1 medium sweet potato, cut into thin sticks
- 1 tablespoon olive oil
- ½ teaspoon dried parsley
- ¼ teaspoon garlic powder
- Salt and pepper to taste

For the Homemade Ketchup:
- ½ cup diced tomatoes
- ¼ cup tomato paste
- 1 tablespoon apple cider vinegar
- 1 tablespoon brown sugar
- ½ teaspoon paprika
- Pinch of ground cloves
- Pinch of salt

Instructions

1. Preheat your Breville Smart Air Fryer Oven Pro to 400°F (200°C).
2. In a large bowl, toss the potato and sweet potato sticks with olive oil, parsley, garlic powder, salt, and pepper. Ensure all fries are evenly coated.
3. Arrange the veggie fries in a single layer on the air fryer basket, ensuring they don't touch. You may need to cook them in batches depending on the size of your air fryer basket.
4. Air fry for 20-25 minutes, or until the fries are golden brown and crispy, flipping them halfway through cooking for even browning.

For the Homemade Ketchup

1. In a small saucepan, combine diced tomatoes, tomato paste, apple cider vinegar, brown sugar, paprika, cloves, and salt.
2. Bring the mixture to a simmer over medium heat, then reduce heat and simmer for 10 minutes, or until slightly thickened.
3. Remove from heat and let cool slightly before blending until smooth using an immersion blender or a regular blender.

Tips

- Soak the potato and sweet potato sticks in cold water for 30 minutes before air frying to help them crisp up. Just be sure to pat them dry completely before adding them to the air fryer.
- Feel free to use other vegetables like carrots, zucchini, or bell peppers for your veggie fries.
- You can adjust the sweetness and tang of the homemade ketchup to your preference.

Nutritional Information (per serving)

Calories: 250 for Veggie Fries only),
Fat: 5g, **Protein**: 2g, **Carbs**: 40g

These air-fried veggie fries are a fun and healthy alternative to traditional potato fries.

Alex & Jamie
Blake

SERVES	PREP TIME	COOK TIME
4	15 minutes	15 - 20 minutes

AIR-FRIED ONION RINGS

Ingredients

- 1 large onion, sliced into ½ inch thick rings
- 1 cup all-purpose flour
- ½ cup cornstarch
- 1 teaspoon baking powder
- ½ teaspoon garlic powder
- ½ teaspoon paprika
- 1 teaspoon dried thyme (optional)
- 1 cup buttermilk
- 2 cups panko breadcrumbs
- Cooking spray
- Salt and pepper to taste

Instructions

1. Preheat your Breville Smart Air Fryer Oven Pro to 400°F (200°C). Lightly grease the air fryer basket with cooking spray.
2. In a shallow bowl, whisk together the flour, cornstarch, baking powder, garlic powder, paprika, and thyme (if using). Season with salt and pepper to taste.
3. In another shallow bowl, pour the buttermilk. In a third shallow bowl, place the panko breadcrumbs.
4. Separate the onion rings, ensuring they are not stuck together. Dredge each onion ring in the flour mixture, coating it evenly. Dip it next in the buttermilk, ensuring complete coverage. Finally, roll the onion ring in the panko breadcrumbs, pressing gently to adhere the crumbs.
5. Place the breaded onion rings in a single layer in the air fryer basket, ensuring they don't touch. You may need to cook them in batches depending on the size of your air fryer basket.
6. Air fry for 15-20 minutes, or until golden brown and crispy on the outside, and the onion is tender on the inside. Flip the onion rings halfway through cooking for even browning.
7. Serve hot with your favorite dipping sauce like marinara sauce, ranch dressing, or a creamy horseradish sauce.

Tips

- Soak the sliced onions in cold water for 10 minutes before breading to help remove some of the sharpness. Pat them dry completely before proceeding.
- Use a mandoline slicer for even and uniform onion rings.
- For an extra cheesy twist, sprinkle the breaded onion rings with grated Parmesan cheese before air frying.

Alex & Jamie
Blake

Nutritional Information (per serving)

Calories: 300, **Fat**: 12g,
Protein: 5g, **Carbs**: 35g

These air-fried onion rings, offering a satisfying crunch without the excess grease.

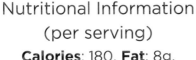

SERVES
4

PREP TIME
5 minutes

COOK TIME
12 - 15 minutes

SPICY BAKED EDAMAME

Ingredients

- 2 (12 oz) packages frozen edamame pods, in the shell
- 1 tablespoon olive oil
- 1 teaspoon sriracha sauce (adjust to your spice preference)
- ½ teaspoon garlic powder
- ¼ teaspoon smoked paprika
- Salt and pepper to taste

Instructions

1. Preheat your Breville Smart Air Fryer Oven Pro to 400°F (200°C).
2. In a large bowl, toss the frozen edamame pods with olive oil, sriracha sauce, garlic powder, smoked paprika, salt, and pepper. Ensure all edamame pods are evenly coated.
3. Spread the edamame pods in a single layer on the air fryer basket.
4. Air fry for 12-15 minutes, or until the edamame pods are heated through and the shells are slightly blistered. Shake the basket occasionally for even browning.
5. Let the edamame cool slightly before serving. Sprinkle with additional chili flakes or serve with a lime wedge for extra flavor.

Tips

- Thaw the frozen edamame pods for a few minutes before air frying for faster cooking.
- You can substitute olive oil with avocado oil for a healthy fat alternative.
- Experiment with different spices and herbs like Cajun seasoning, Everything Bagel Seasoning, or a sprinkle of furikake for a variety of flavor profiles.

Nutritional Information
(per serving)
Calories: 180, **Fat**: 8g,
Protein: 17g, **Carbs**: 10g

This air-fried edamame is a protein-rich and flavorful snack option with a touch of heat.

SERVES	PREP TIME	COOK TIME
4	15 minutes	15 - 20 minutes

AIR-FRIED MINI QUICHES

Ingredients

- 1 sheet frozen puff pastry, thawed
- 4 large eggs
- ¼ cup milk (dairy or non-dairy)
- ¼ cup shredded cheddar cheese
- ¼ cup crumbled feta cheese
- ¼ cup chopped cooked ham or crumbled cooked bacon (optional)
- ¼ cup chopped vegetables (chopped onion, bell peppers, spinach, mushrooms)
- Salt and pepper to taste

Instructions

1. Preheat your Breville Smart Air Fryer Oven Pro to 375°F (190°C) using the bake function. Lightly grease a mini muffin tin with cooking spray.
2. Unfold the thawed puff pastry sheet and cut it into 12 squares. Gently press each square into the greased mini muffin cups, forming a well.
3. In a large bowl, whisk together the eggs, milk, salt, and pepper.
4. Stir in the shredded cheddar cheese, crumbled feta cheese, chopped cooked ham or bacon (if using), and chopped vegetables.
5. Fill each puff pastry cup with the egg mixture, ensuring it doesn't overflow.
6. Air fry for 15-20 minutes, or until the egg filling is set and the crust is golden brown. You can insert a toothpick into the center of a quiche; it should come out clean when the quiches are done.
7. Let the mini quiches cool slightly before serving. Enjoy them warm or at room temperature.

Tips

- Feel free to experiment with different fillings for your mini quiches. Chopped broccoli, sun-dried tomatoes, or chopped cooked sausage are great alternatives.
- You can prepare the mini quiches ahead of time and assemble them in the muffin tin. Cover them with plastic wrap and refrigerate overnight. Simply air fry them in the morning for a quick and easy snack.
- For a vegetarian option, omit the ham or bacon and add additional vegetables like chopped mushrooms or spinach.

Alex & Jamie Blake

Nutritional Information (per serving)

Calories: 200, **Fat**: 12g, **Protein**: 8g, **Carbs**: 15g

These bite-sized quiches are perfect for a savory snack or light lunch.

SERVES
4

 PREP TIME
10 minutes

 COOK TIME
8 - 10 minutes

CRISPY AIR-FRIED WONTONS

Ingredients

- 1 (32 oz) package wonton wrappers
- 1 tablespoon vegetable oil
- Salt and pepper to taste
- Optional fillings: Chopped cooked chicken, shredded pork, diced vegetables (carrots, peas, cabbage)

Instructions

1. Preheat your Breville Smart Air Fryer Oven Pro to 400°F (200°C). Lightly grease the air fryer basket with cooking spray.
2. If using fillings, prepare them beforehand and place a small spoonful in the center of each wonton wrapper.
3. Brush the edges of the wonton wrapper with a little vegetable oil or water to help seal them. Fold the wonton wrapper diagonally to form a triangle, then fold the corners down towards the center to create a pouch shape. You can also fold them into little purses or any desired shape.
4. Arrange the wontons in a single layer in the air fryer basket, ensuring they don't touch. You may need to cook them in batches depending on the size of your air fryer basket.
5. Air fry for 8-10 minutes, or until golden brown and crispy. Shake the basket occasionally for even browning.
6. Serve hot with your favorite dipping sauces like soy sauce, sweet and sour sauce, or chili oil.

Tips

- Experiment with different fillings for your wontons. Cream cheese wontons with a drizzle of honey or sriracha mayo are delicious options.
- You can use store-bought wonton wrappers or make your own for a more customized experience.
- Feel free to sprinkle the wontons with sesame seeds or chopped scallions before air frying for an extra flavor boost.

Nutritional Information
(per serving)
Calories: 150, **Fat**: 3g,
Protein: 5g, **Carbs**: 25g

These air-fried wontons are a fun and customizable finger food, perfect for dipping in your favorite sauces.

SERVES
4

 PREP TIME
15 minutes

 COOK TIME
10 - 12 minutes

BAKED PARMESAN GARLIC KNOTS

Ingredients

- 1 pound store-bought pizza dough, at room temperature
- 2 tablespoons melted butter
- 2 tablespoons olive oil
- 2 cloves garlic, minced
- ½ cup grated Parmesan cheese
- ¼ teaspoon dried oregano
- Salt and pepper to taste

Instructions

1. Preheat your Breville Smart Air Fryer Oven Pro to 400°F (200°C). Lightly grease the air fryer basket with cooking spray.
2. In a small bowl, combine the melted butter, olive oil, minced garlic, grated Parmesan cheese, oregano, salt, and pepper.
3. Divide the pizza dough into 12 equal pieces. Roll each piece into a long rope-like shape.
4. Tie each rope into a knot and place them in the greased air fryer basket, ensuring they don't touch.
5. Brush the tops of the knots generously with the garlic butter mixture.
6. Air fry for 10-12 minutes, or until golden brown and cooked through.
7. Serve hot with your favorite dipping sauce like marinara sauce or a simple mixture of olive oil and balsamic vinegar.

Tips

- For chewier knots, preheat the air fryer for a few minutes before adding the knots.
- If your knots start to brown too quickly on top, tent them loosely with a piece of aluminum foil for the last few minutes of cooking.
- Feel free to sprinkle the knots with additional grated Parmesan cheese or chopped fresh parsley before serving.

Alex & Jamie
Blake

Nutritional Information
(per serving)
Calories: 300, **Fat**: 15g,
Protein: 8g, **Carbs**: 30g

These air-fried parmesan garlic knots are a delicious alternative to traditional breadsticks.

| SERVES 4 | PREP TIME 15 minutes | COOK TIME 5 - 7 minutes |

AIR-FRIED CINNAMON SUGAR DONUT HOLES

Ingredients

- 1 cup all-purpose flour
- 2 teaspoons baking powder
- ½ teaspoon salt
- ¼ cup granulated sugar
- ¼ cup milk (dairy or non-dairy)
- 1 tablespoon melted butter
- 1 teaspoon vanilla extract
- Canola oil for frying (optional)

For the cinnamon sugar coating:

- ½ cup granulated sugar
- 1 teaspoon ground cinnamon

Instructions

1. In a large bowl, whisk together the flour, baking powder, and salt.
2. In a separate bowl, whisk together the granulated sugar, milk, melted butter, and vanilla extract.
3. Combine the wet ingredients with the dry ingredients, mixing until just combined. A shaggy dough will form.
4. On a lightly floured surface, knead the dough for a minute or two until smooth.
5. Roll out the dough to a ¼ inch thickness. Use a donut cutter or a small round cookie cutter to cut out donut holes.
6. If desired, heat a few inches of canola oil in a deep skillet or pot over medium heat to 350°F (175°C). Carefully fry the donut holes for 1-2 minutes per side, or until golden brown. Drain on paper towels.
7. Preheat your Breville Smart Air Fryer Oven Pro to 375°F (190°C) (or preheat to 400°F (200°C) if you haven't fried the donut holes). In a shallow bowl, combine the granulated sugar and cinnamon to create the cinnamon sugar coating.
8. Lightly coat the plain or fried donut holes in the cinnamon sugar mixture.
9. Place the donut holes in a single layer in the air fryer basket, ensuring they don't touch. Air fry for 5-7 minutes, or until warmed through.
10. Serve hot and enjoy!

Tips

- You can freeze the uncooked donut holes for later.
- Feel free to experiment with different coatings for your donut holes. Melted chocolate or a powdered sugar glaze are delicious options.

Nutritional Information (per serving)

Calories: 200, **Fat**: 5g, **Protein**: 2g, **Carbs**: 35g

These air-fried donut holes are a healthier and lighter alternative to deep-fried donuts.

MEAT MARVELS
TENDER AND JUICY AIR-FRIED DELIGHTS WITH THE BREVILLE SMART AIR FRYER OVEN PRO

Unleash the power of your Breville Smart Air Fryer Oven Pro and discover a world of perfectly cooked, juicy meats! This chapter celebrates the versatility of this appliance, showcasing ten delicious recipes that transform ordinary cuts into tender and flavorful masterpieces. From sizzling steaks to herb-infused chicken and savory meatballs, these air-fried creations guarantee a satisfying meal, all without the mess of traditional methods.

Alex & Jamie
Blake

SERVES
1

PREP TIME
5 minutes

COOK TIME
10 - 15 minutes

AIR-FRIED RIBEYE STEAK

Ingredients

- 1 (12 oz) ribeye steak, at least 1 inch thick
- 1 tablespoon olive oil
- 1 teaspoon kosher salt
- ½ teaspoon freshly ground black pepper

Instructions

1. Preheat your Breville Smart Air Fryer Oven Pro to 400°F (200°C) using the "Air Fry" function. Pat the ribeye steak dry with paper towels to remove any surface moisture.
2. In a small bowl, combine olive oil, salt, and pepper. Rub the seasoning mixture generously all over the steak.
3. Place the steak in the preheated air fryer basket, ensuring it doesn't touch the sides.
4. Cook for the following times according to your desired doneness:
5. Rare: 4-5 minutes per side (internal temperature 125°F (52°C))
6. Medium-rare: 5-6 minutes per side (internal temperature 135°F (57°C))
7. Medium: 6-7 minutes per side (internal temperature 145°F (63°C))
8. Medium-well: 7-8 minutes per side (internal temperature 155°F (68°C))
9. Well-done: 8-9 minutes per side (internal temperature 160°F (71°C))
10. Use a meat thermometer to check the internal temperature of the steak for accuracy.
11. Once cooked to your desired doneness, transfer the steak to a plate and let it rest for 5 minutes before slicing. This allows the juices to redistribute throughout the meat, resulting in a more tender and flavorful experience.
12. Serve immediately with your favorite sides like roasted vegetables, mashed potatoes, or a simple salad.

Tips

- For a thicker steak (over 1.5 inches), increase the cooking time by 2-3 minutes per side for each desired level of doneness.
- You can experiment with different seasonings like garlic powder, smoked paprika, or a steak rub for additional flavor variations.

Nutritional Information (per serving)
Calories: 600, **Fat**: 40g,
Protein: 50g, **Carbs**: 0g

This recipe delivers a restaurant-quality ribeye steak, cooked to your desired doneness, with a beautifully caramelized crust.

29

| SERVES 4 | PREP TIME 10 minutes | COOK TIME 15 - 20 minutes |

HERB-ROASTED AIR-FRIED CHICKEN BREASTS

Ingredients

- 4 boneless, skinless chicken breasts (around 6 oz each)
- 2 tablespoons olive oil
- 1 tablespoon dried thyme
- 1 teaspoon dried rosemary
- ½ teaspoon garlic powder
- ½ teaspoon onion powder
- Salt and freshly ground black pepper to taste

Instructions

1. Preheat your Breville Smart Air Fryer Oven Pro to 400°F (200°C) using the "Air Fry" function.
2. In a shallow bowl, combine olive oil, thyme, rosemary, garlic powder, onion powder, salt, and pepper.
3. Pat the chicken breasts dry with paper towels.
4. Place the chicken breasts in the olive oil mixture and coat them evenly with the seasoning.
5. Arrange the chicken breasts in a single layer in the air fryer basket, ensuring they don't touch.
6. Air fry for 15-20 minutes, or until the chicken breasts are cooked through and the internal temperature reaches 165°F (74°C). Flip the chicken breasts halfway through cooking for even browning.
7. Let the chicken breasts rest for 5 minutes before slicing and serving

Alex & Jamie
Blake

Nutritional Information
(per serving)
Calories: 250, **Fat**: 5g,
Protein: 40g, **Carbs**: 0g

These air-fried chicken breasts are juicy, flavorful, and incredibly easy to make.

| | SERVES 4 | | PREP TIME 15 minutes | | COOK TIME 15 - 20 minutes |

AIR-FRIED PORK CHOPS WITH HONEY MUSTARD GLAZE

Alex & Jamie Blake

Ingredients

- 4 bone-in pork chops (around 1 inch thick)
- 1 tablespoon olive oil
- 1 teaspoon dried oregano
- ½ teaspoon garlic powder
- ½ teaspoon onion powder
- Salt and freshly ground black pepper to taste

For the Honey Mustard Glaze:
- 2 tablespoons Dijon mustard
- 1 tablespoon honey
- 1 tablespoon soy sauce
- 1 tablespoon apple cider vinegar

Instructions

1. Preheat your Breville Smart Air Fryer Oven Pro to 400°F (200°C) using the "Air Fry" function. Pat the pork chops dry with paper towels.
2. In a shallow bowl, combine olive oil, oregano, garlic powder, onion powder, salt, and pepper. Season the pork chops generously with the spice mixture, ensuring all sides are coated.
3. **For the Honey Mustard Glaze**: In a small bowl, whisk together Dijon mustard, honey, soy sauce, and apple cider vinegar until well combined.
4. Place the pork chops in a single layer in the air fryer basket, ensuring they don't touch.
5. Air fry for 10 minutes.
6. While the pork chops are cooking, brush them generously with half of the honey mustard glaze.
7. Continue air frying for another 5-10 minutes, or until the pork chops are cooked through and the internal temperature reaches 145°F (63°C). Brush the pork chops with the remaining glaze during the last few minutes of cooking for a sticky and flavorful glaze.
8. Let the pork chops rest for 5 minutes before serving.

Tips

- Use a meat thermometer to ensure the pork chops reach the proper internal temperature for safe consumption.
- Thicker pork chops (over 1 inch) may require additional cooking time. Check for doneness after 15 minutes and continue cooking in 2-minute increments if needed.
- For a spicier glaze, add a pinch of red pepper flakes to the honey mustard mixture.

Nutritional Information (per serving)
Calories: 400, **Fat**: 25g, **Protein**: 40g, **Carbs**: 5g

These air-fried pork chops are incredibly flavorful and come together with a sweet and tangy honey mustard glaze.

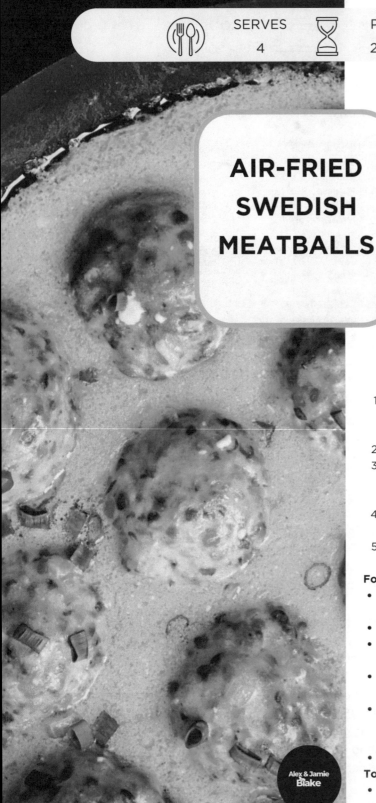

| SERVES 4 | PREP TIME 20 minutes | COOK TIME 15 - 20 minutes |

AIR-FRIED SWEDISH MEATBALLS

Ingredients

- 1 pound ground beef
- ½ cup panko breadcrumbs
- ¼ cup grated onion
- 1 tablespoon milk (dairy or non-dairy)
- 1 large egg, beaten
- 1 teaspoon Worcestershire sauce
- ½ teaspoon dried thyme
- Salt and freshly ground black pepper to taste

For the Sauce:
- 1 tablespoon olive oil
- 1 tablespoon butter
- 1 tablespoon all-purpose flour
- 1 cup beef broth
- ½ cup heavy cream (or unsweetened almond milk for a dairy-free option)
- 1 tablespoon brown sugar
- 1 tablespoon tomato paste
- ½ teaspoon dried parsley

Instructions

1. In a large bowl, combine ground beef, panko breadcrumbs, grated onion, milk, beaten egg, Worcestershire sauce, thyme, salt, and pepper. Mix well until everything is evenly combined.
2. Form the mixture into small meatballs, around 1 inch in diameter.
3. Preheat your Breville Smart Air Fryer Oven Pro to 400°F (200°C) using the "Air Fry" function. Lightly grease the air fryer basket with cooking spray.
4. Arrange the meatballs in a single layer in the air fryer basket, ensuring they don't touch.
5. Air fry for 15-20 minutes, or until the meatballs are cooked through and golden brown.

For the Sauce:
- While the meatballs are air frying, heat olive oil and butter in a saucepan over medium heat.
- Whisk in the flour and cook for 1 minute, stirring constantly.
- Slowly whisk in the beef broth, scraping up any browned bits from the bottom of the pan.
- Bring to a simmer and cook for 5 minutes, or until the sauce thickens slightly.
- Stir in heavy cream (or unsweetened almond milk), brown sugar, tomato paste, and dried parsley. Season with salt and pepper to taste.
- Simmer for an additional 2-3 minutes, or until the flavors meld.

To Serve:
- Once the meatballs are cooked through, transfer them to a serving dish.
- Pour the warm sauce over the meatballs and garnish with chopped fresh parsley (optional).
- Serve with mashed potatoes, egg noodles, or your favorite side dish.

Nutritional Information (per serving)

Calories: 400, (without sauce)
Fat: 20g, **Protein**: 30g, **Carbs**: 25g

These air-fried Swedish meatballs are a lighter and healthier take on the classic comfort food.

SERVES 4   **PREP TIME** 15 minutes   **COOK TIME** 20 - 25 minutes

AIR-FRIED CAJUN PORK TENDERLOIN WITH SPICY REMOULADE

Ingredients

- 1 (1-1.5 pound) pork tenderloin, trimmed of any excess fat
- 1 tablespoon olive oil
- 1 teaspoon paprika
- ½ teaspoon cayenne pepper (adjust to your spice preference)
- ½ teaspoon garlic powder
- ½ teaspoon onion powder
- Salt and freshly ground black pepper to taste

For the Spicy Remoulade:
- ½ cup mayonnaise
- 1 tablespoon Dijon mustard
- 1 tablespoon ketchup
- 1 tablespoon chopped green onion
- 1 tablespoon chopped fresh parsley
- 1 teaspoon lemon juice
- ½ teaspoon hot sauce (adjust to your spice preference)
- Pinch of paprika
- Salt and freshly ground black pepper to taste

Instructions

1. Preheat your Breville Smart Air Fryer Oven Pro to 400°F (200°C) using the "Air Fry" function. Pat the pork tenderloin dry with paper towels.
2. In a shallow bowl, combine olive oil, paprika, cayenne pepper, garlic powder, onion powder, salt, and pepper. Rub the spice mixture generously all over the pork tenderloin, ensuring it's well coated.
3. For the Spicy Remoulade: In a small bowl, whisk together mayonnaise, Dijon mustard, ketchup, green onion, parsley, lemon juice, hot sauce, paprika, salt, and pepper.
4. Place the pork tenderloin in the air fryer basket, ensuring it doesn't touch the sides.
5. Air fry for 20-25 minutes, or until the internal temperature of the pork tenderloin reaches 145°F (63°C) for safe consumption. Use a meat thermometer to check for accuracy.
6. During the last 5 minutes of cooking, you can brush the pork tenderloin with a little additional olive oil for extra browning (optional).

To Serve:
- Let the pork tenderloin rest for 5 minutes before slicing.
- Serve the sliced pork tenderloin with the spicy remoulade for dipping.
- You can pair this dish with roasted vegetables, mashed potatoes, or rice for a complete meal.

Tips
- Marinate the pork tenderloin in the Cajun spice mixture for at least 30 minutes before air frying for even deeper flavor.

Nutritional Information
(per serving)
Calories: 450, **Fat**: 25g, **Protein**: 40g, **Carbs**: 5g

This recipe brings the vibrant flavors of Cajun cuisine to your air fryer with a succulent pork tenderloin and a creamy remoulade sauce.

AIR-FRIED ASIAN-GLAZED CHICKEN WINGS

Ingredients

- 1 pound chicken wings, separated into wingettes and drumettes
- 1 tablespoon soy sauce
- 1 tablespoon rice vinegar
- 1 tablespoon brown sugar
- 1 tablespoon honey
- 1 tablespoon sriracha (adjust to your spice preference)
- 1 teaspoon grated ginger
- 1 clove garlic, minced
- ½ teaspoon sesame oil

Instructions

1. Preheat your Breville Smart Air Fryer Oven Pro to 400°F (200°C) using the "Air Fry" function. Pat the chicken wings dry with paper towels.
2. In a shallow bowl, whisk together soy sauce, rice vinegar, brown sugar, honey, sriracha, ginger, garlic, and sesame oil.
3. Toss the chicken wings in the glaze mixture to coat them evenly.
4. Arrange the chicken wings in a single layer in the air fryer basket, ensuring they don't touch.
5. Air fry for 20 minutes.
6. While the chicken wings are cooking, prepare a bowl with a few tablespoons of the remaining glaze.
7. After 20 minutes, flip the chicken wings and brush them generously with the reserved glaze.
8. Continue air frying for an additional 5-10 minutes, or until the chicken wings are cooked through and crispy. The glaze should be sticky and caramelized.
9. Serve the chicken wings hot with your favorite dipping sauce like blue cheese dressing or ranch dressing.

Tips

- For extra crispy wings, pat the chicken wings dry thoroughly before tossing them in the glaze.
- Marinate the chicken wings in the glaze for at least 30 minutes before air frying for even deeper flavor.
- You can adjust the amount of sriracha in the glaze to suit your spice preference.

Nutritional Information (per serving)

Calories: 500, **Fat**: 30g, **Protein**: 40g, **Carbs**: 10g

These air-fried chicken wings are crispy on the outside and incredibly flavorful with a sticky Asian-inspired glaze.

SERVES	PREP TIME	COOK TIME
4	15 minutes	30 - 35 minutes

AIR-FRIED CHIPOTLE CHICKEN THIGHS

Ingredients

- 4 bone-in, skin-on chicken thighs (around 1 pound each)
- 2 tablespoons olive oil
- 1 tablespoon chipotle chili powder
- 1 teaspoon smoked paprika
- 1 teaspoon cumin
- ½ teaspoon garlic powder
- ½ teaspoon onion powder
- Salt and freshly ground black pepper to taste
- 1 lime, juiced (optional)

Instructions

1. Preheat your Breville Smart Air Fryer Oven Pro to 400°F (200°C) using the "Air Fry" function. Pat the chicken thighs dry with paper towels.
2. In a shallow bowl, combine olive oil, chipotle chili powder, smoked paprika, cumin, garlic powder, onion powder, salt, and pepper.
3. Rub the spice mixture generously all over the chicken thighs, ensuring they are well coated.
4. Place the chicken thighs skin-side up in a single layer in the air fryer basket, ensuring they don't touch.
5. Air fry for 30-35 minutes, or until the chicken thighs are cooked through and the juices run clear when pierced with a fork. The skin should be crispy and golden brown.
6. During the last 5 minutes of cooking, you can brush the chicken thighs with lime juice for an extra burst of flavor (optional).

Tips

- Use a meat thermometer to ensure the chicken thighs reach an internal temperature of 165°F (74°C) for safe consumption.
- For thicker chicken thighs, increase the cooking time by 5-10 minutes.
- Leftover chipotle chicken thighs can be shredded and used in tacos, burritos, or salads.

Alex & Jamie
Blake

Nutritional Information (per serving)

Calories: 500, **Fat**: 35g,
Protein: 45g, **Carbs**: 5g

These air-fried chipotle chicken thighs are bursting with smoky and spicy flavors, perfect for a flavorful and satisfying meal.

AIR-FRIED LAMB CHOPS WITH MINT PESTO

Ingredients

- 2 bone-in lamb chops (around 1 inch thick)
- 1 tablespoon olive oil
- Salt and freshly ground black pepper to taste

For the Mint Pesto:
- 1 cup packed fresh mint leaves
- ½ cup grated Parmesan cheese
- ¼ cup pine nuts
- 2 cloves garlic
- 1 tablespoon olive oil
- Salt and freshly ground black pepper to taste

Instructions

1. Preheat your Breville Smart Air Fryer Oven Pro to 400°F (200°C) using the "Air Fry" function. Pat the lamb chops dry with paper towels. Season them generously with salt and freshly ground black pepper.
2. **For the Mint Pesto:** In a food processor, combine mint leaves, Parmesan cheese, pine nuts, garlic, and olive oil. Pulse until a coarse pesto forms. Season with salt and pepper to taste.
3. Place the lamb chops in a single layer in the air fryer basket, ensuring they don't touch.
4. Air fry for 10-12 minutes, or until the lamb chops are cooked to your desired doneness. Here's a guideline:
- Rare: 4-5 minutes per side - internal temperature 125°F (52°C)
- Medium-rare: 5-6 minutes per side - internal temperature 135°F (57°C)
- Medium: 6-7 minutes per side - internal temperature 145°F (63°C)
5. Use a meat thermometer to check the internal temperature of the lamb chops for accuracy.
6. Once cooked, transfer the lamb chops to a plate and let them rest for 5 minutes before serving.
7. Spoon the mint pesto over the lamb chops and enjoy!

Optional (Making Pesto with Mortar and Pestle):
- If you don't have a food processor, you can make the pesto using a mortar and pestle.
- Finely grind the garlic and pine nuts in the mortar.
- Add the mint leaves and continue grinding until fragrant.
- Stir in the Parmesan cheese and olive oil, and season with salt and pepper.

Nutritional Information (per serving)

Calories: 600, **Fat**: 40g, **Protein**: 50g, **Carbs**: 5g

This recipe showcases the versatility of your air fryer with succulent lamb chops and a vibrant homemade mint pesto.

SERVES 4	PREP TIME 15 minutes	COOK TIME 10 - 12 minutes

AIR-FRIED GARLIC HERB BEEF BURGERS

Ingredients

- 1 pound ground beef (80/20 lean-to-fat ratio)
- 1 tablespoon olive oil
- 1 teaspoon Worcestershire sauce
- ½ teaspoon garlic powder
- ½ teaspoon onion powder
- ½ teaspoon dried thyme
- Salt and freshly ground black pepper to taste
- Hamburger buns (toasted, optional)
- Your favorite burger toppings (cheese, lettuce, tomato, onion, etc.)

Instructions

1. Preheat your Breville Smart Air Fryer Oven Pro to 400°F (200°C) using the "Air Fry" function.
2. In a large bowl, combine ground beef, olive oil, Worcestershire sauce, garlic powder, onion powder, thyme, salt, and pepper. Mix well to combine.
3. Gently form the mixture into 4 equal-sized patties.
4. Lightly grease the air fryer basket with cooking spray.
5. Place the burgers in a single layer in the air fryer basket, ensuring they don't touch.
6. Air fry for 10-12 minutes, or until the burgers are cooked through to your desired doneness. An internal temperature of 160°F (71°C) is recommended for safe consumption. Flip the burgers halfway through cooking for even browning.

Tips

- For thicker burgers, increase the cooking time by 2-3 minutes per side.
- You can use a burger press to create uniform patties.
- Toast your hamburger buns in the Breville Smart Air Fryer Oven Pro using the "Bake" function for a few minutes before assembling your burgers.
- Get creative with your toppings! Experiment with different cheeses, vegetables, and sauces to find your perfect burger combination.

Alex & Jamie
Blake

Nutritional Information
(per serving)

Calories: 450, **Fat**: 30g, **Protein**: 40g, **Carbs**: 5g (without bun)

These air-fried burgers are juicy, flavorful, and perfect for a quick and easy weeknight meal.

SERVES
4 - 6

 PREP TIME
10 minutes

 COOK TIME
5 - 7 minutes

AIR-FRIED SMOKY BBQ BEEF BRISKET SLIDERS

Ingredients

- 1 pound leftover cooked beef brisket, thinly sliced
- ½ cup barbecue sauce (your favorite brand or homemade)
- 2 tablespoons Worcestershire sauce
- 1 tablespoon Dijon mustard
- Hamburger buns or slider buns
- Optional toppings: coleslaw, pickles, red onion

Instructions

1. Preheat your Breville Smart Air Fryer Oven Pro to 400°F (200°C) using the "Air Fry" function.
2. In a shallow bowl, combine barbecue sauce, Worcestershire sauce, and Dijon mustard. Whisk to create a smooth sauce.
3. Toss the sliced beef brisket in the barbecue sauce mixture to coat them evenly.
4. Arrange the brisket slices in a single layer in the air fryer basket, ensuring they don't touch.
5. Air fry for 5-7 minutes, or until the brisket is heated through and the barbecue sauce is bubbly and slightly caramelized.

To Assemble Sliders:

6. Toast the hamburger buns or slider buns in the Breville Smart Air Fryer Oven Pro using the "Toast" function for a few minutes, or until lightly toasted (optional).
7. Place a warmed bun on a plate and top it with a slice of air-fried brisket.
8. Add your favorite toppings like coleslaw, pickles, and red onion for an extra burst of flavor and texture.

Tips

- If your leftover brisket is thick, you may need to cut it even thinner for easier air frying.
- You can adjust the amount of barbecue sauce to your preference.
- For a spicier flavor, add a pinch of cayenne pepper to the barbecue sauce mixture.
- Leftover air-fried brisket sliders can be stored in an airtight container in the refrigerator for up to 3 days. Reheat them gently in the air fryer for a few minutes.

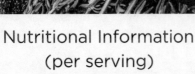

Alex & Jamie
Blake

Nutritional Information
(per serving)
Calories: (varies), **Fat**: (varies), **Protein**: (varies), **Carbs**: (varies)

This recipe transforms leftover beef brisket into delicious and smoky air-fried sliders.

SEAFOOD SENSATIONS

UNVEILING FLAVORFUL AIR-FRIED DELIGHTS WITH THE BREVILLE SMART AIR FRYER OVEN PRO

Dive into a world of vibrant flavors and healthy cooking with this chapter showcasing ten delectable seafood recipes made possible by the Breville Smart Air Fryer Oven Pro. From golden-brown fish and chips to herb-infused salmon and succulent shrimp scampi, these air-fried creations unlock a new level of convenience and taste for your favorite seafood dishes.

Alex & Jamie Blake

AIR-FRIED CRISPY FISH AND CHIPS

Ingredients

- 2 (4 oz) cod fillets
- ½ cup all-purpose flour
- 1 teaspoon paprika
- ½ teaspoon garlic powder
- ½ teaspoon onion powder
- Salt and freshly ground black pepper to taste
- 1 large russet potato, cut into wedges
- 1 tablespoon olive oil

Instructions

1. Preheat your Breville Smart Air Fryer Oven Pro to 400°F (200°C) using the "Air Fry" function.
2. Pat the cod fillets dry with paper towels. Season them generously with salt and pepper.
3. In a shallow bowl, combine flour, paprika, garlic powder, and onion powder. Dredge the cod fillets in the seasoned flour mixture, ensuring they are evenly coated.
4. Cut the russet potato into wedges, aiming for similar thickness for even cooking. Toss the potato wedges with olive oil, salt, and pepper.
5. Arrange the breaded cod fillets and potato wedges in a single layer in the air fryer basket, ensuring they don't touch.
6. Air fry for 20-25 minutes, or until the fish is cooked through and flakes easily with a fork, and the potato wedges are golden brown and crisp. Flip the potato wedges halfway through cooking for even browning.

Tips

- Use a light and flaky white fish like cod, haddock, or tilapia for this recipe.
- If your air fryer basket is small, you may need to cook the fish and potato wedges in batches.
- Serve the air-fried fish and chips with tartar sauce, malt vinegar, or your favorite dipping sauce.

Nutritional Information (per serving)

Calories: 500, **Fat**: 20g,
Protein: 40g, **Carbs**: 40g

This classic comfort food gets a healthier makeover with perfectly crispy fish and golden potato wedges, all prepared in your air fryer.

AIR-FRIED SALMON WITH LEMON AND HERBS

Ingredients

- 2 (6 oz) salmon fillets (skin-on or skinless, depending on preference)
- 1 tablespoon olive oil
- 1 tablespoon lemon juice
- 1 teaspoon dried thyme
- ½ teaspoon dried rosemary
- Salt and freshly ground black pepper to taste
- Fresh herbs (optional): Chopped parsley, dill, or chives for garnish

Instructions

1. Preheat your Breville Smart Air Fryer Oven Pro to 400°F (200°C) using the "Air Fry" function. Pat the salmon fillets dry with paper towels.
2. In a shallow bowl, combine olive oil, lemon juice, thyme, rosemary, salt, and pepper.
3. Place the salmon fillets in a single layer in the air fryer basket. Brush the top of the salmon with the lemon herb mixture.
4. Air fry for 12-15 minutes, or until the salmon is cooked through and flakes easily with a fork. The internal temperature should reach 145°F (63°C) for safe consumption.
5. (Optional) During the last few minutes of cooking, you can brush the salmon with some additional lemon herb mixture for extra flavor and a glossy finish.

Tips

- Use fresh lemon juice for the best flavor.
- You can substitute fresh herbs like thyme, rosemary, dill, or parsley for the dried ones.
- Serve the air-fried salmon with roasted vegetables, quinoa, or rice for a complete meal.
- Garnish with fresh chopped parsley, dill, or chives before serving for an extra touch of elegance.

Nutritional Information (per serving)

Calories: 400, **Fat**: 25g,
Protein: 45g, **Carbs**: 0g

This recipe delivers a restaurant-worthy salmon dish with a burst of citrusy lemon and fragrant herbs, all prepared in your air fryer with minimal fuss.

AIR-FRIED GARLIC BUTTER SHRIMP SCAMPI

Ingredients

- 1 pound large shrimp, peeled and deveined (tails on or off, depending on preference)
- 2 tablespoons olive oil
- 4 tablespoons butter
- 4 cloves garlic, minced
- ½ teaspoon dried parsley
- ½ teaspoon dried oregano
- Salt and freshly ground black pepper to taste
- 1 tablespoon lemon juice (optional)
- Fresh parsley, chopped (for garnish)

Instructions

1. Preheat your Breville Smart Air Fryer Oven Pro to 400°F (200°C) using the "Air Fry" function. Pat the shrimp dry with paper towels.
2. In a shallow bowl, combine olive oil, melted butter, garlic, parsley, oregano, salt, and pepper. Toss the shrimp in the mixture to coat them evenly.
3. Arrange the shrimp in a single layer in the air fryer basket, ensuring they don't touch.
4. Air fry for 5-7 minutes, or until the shrimp are pink and opaque throughout. The shrimp should be cooked through and slightly firm to the touch.
5. (Optional) During the last minute of cooking, drizzle the shrimp with lemon juice for a touch of acidity (optional).

Tips

- For larger shrimp, adjust the cooking time by 1-2 minutes.
- You can use frozen shrimp for this recipe, but thaw them completely and pat them dry before air frying.
- Serve the air-fried scampi over pasta, rice, or with crusty bread for dipping in the delicious garlic butter sauce.
- Garnish with fresh chopped parsley for an extra pop of color and flavor.

Alex & Jamie Blake

Nutritional Information (per serving)

Calories: 450, **Fat**: 30g, **Protein**: 40g, **Carbs**: 5g

This recipe brings the essence of a classic scampi dish to your air fryer, featuring succulent shrimp bathed in a rich garlic butter sauce.

SERVES
4

 PREP TIME
15 minutes

 **COOK TIME**
15 - 20 minutes

AIR-FRIED COCONUT CURRY SHRIMP WITH VEGETABLES

Ingredients

- 1 pound medium shrimp, peeled and deveined
- 1 tablespoon olive oil
- 1 teaspoon curry powder
- ½ teaspoon turmeric powder
- ½ teaspoon ground ginger
- ¼ teaspoon red pepper flakes (adjust to your spice preference)
- 1 (13.5 oz) can coconut milk
- ½ cup chopped vegetables (broccoli, bell peppers, carrots, etc.)
- Salt and freshly ground black pepper to taste
- Fresh cilantro, chopped (for garnish)

Instructions

1. Preheat your Breville Smart Air Fryer Oven Pro to 400°F (200°C) using the "Air Fry" function. Pat the shrimp dry with paper towels.
2. In a shallow bowl, combine olive oil, curry powder, turmeric powder, ginger, and red pepper flakes. Toss the shrimp in the spice mixture to coat them evenly.
3. In a separate bowl, toss the chopped vegetables with a little olive oil and salt.
4. Arrange the shrimp and vegetables in a single layer in the air fryer basket, ensuring they don't touch.
5. Pour the coconut milk over the shrimp and vegetables.
6. Air fry for 15-20 minutes, or until the shrimp are cooked through and the vegetables are tender-crisp. Stir the mixture halfway through cooking for even distribution of flavors.

Tips

- You can use a pre-made curry paste instead of individual spices for a quicker option.
- Choose your favorite vegetables for this recipe. Broccoli, bell peppers, carrots, and snow peas work well.
- Serve the air-fried coconut curry shrimp with rice or quinoa for a complete meal.
- Garnish with fresh chopped cilantro before serving for an extra touch of freshness.

Alex & Jamie
Blake

Nutritional Information (per serving)
Calories: 400, **Fat**: 20g,
Protein: 35g, **Carbs**: 20g

This recipe offers a taste of the tropics with air-fried shrimp nestled in a fragrant coconut curry sauce with colorful vegetables.

| SERVES 2 | PREP TIME 20 minutes | COOK TIME 15 - 20 minutes |

AIR-FRIED VEGGIE-STUFFED COD

Ingredients

- 2 (6 oz) cod fillets
- ½ cup chopped vegetables (broccoli florets, chopped bell peppers, zucchini, etc.)
- ¼ cup chopped red onion
- 1 clove garlic, minced
- ¼ cup crumbled feta cheese
- 2 tablespoons chopped fresh parsley
- 1 tablespoon olive oil
- Salt and freshly ground black pepper to taste
- 1 tablespoon lemon juice (optional)

Instructions

1. Preheat your Breville Smart Air Fryer Oven Pro to 400°F (200°C) using the "Air Fry" function.
2. Carefully pat the cod fillets dry with paper towels. Using a sharp knife, make a pocket in each fillet by carefully cutting a slit along the thickest part, without cutting all the way through.
3. In a medium bowl, combine chopped vegetables, red onion, garlic, crumbled feta cheese, parsley, olive oil, salt, and pepper. Mix well.
4. Stuff the prepared vegetable mixture into the pockets of the cod fillets.
5. (Optional) Secure the pockets with toothpicks to prevent the filling from spilling out during air frying.
6. Place the stuffed cod fillets in a single layer in the air fryer basket, ensuring they don't touch.
7. Air fry for 15-20 minutes, or until the cod is cooked through and flakes easily with a fork. The internal temperature should reach 145°F (63°C) for safe consumption.
8. During the last few minutes of cooking, you can brush the cod fillets with a little lemon juice for added flavor (optional).

Tips

- You can use a variety of vegetables for the stuffing, such as spinach, mushrooms, or chopped tomatoes.
- If using frozen vegetables, thaw them completely and squeeze out any excess moisture before adding them to the stuffing.

Nutritional Information (per serving)

Calories: 400, **Fat**: 20g, **Protein**: 40g, **Carbs**: 15g

This recipe transforms cod fillets into flavorful pockets filled with a mixture of colorful vegetables and herbs.

SERVES 2   **PREP TIME** 15 minutes   **COOK TIME** 10 - 12 minutes

AIR-FRIED CAJUN MAHI-MAHI WITH REMOULADE

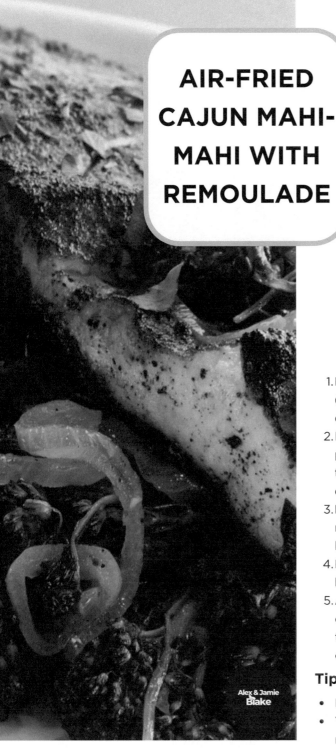

Alex & Jamie **Blake**

Ingredients

- 2 (6 oz) mahi-mahi fillets
- 1 tablespoon olive oil
- 1 teaspoon paprika
- ½ teaspoon cayenne pepper (adjust to your spice preference)
- ½ teaspoon garlic powder
- ½ teaspoon onion powder
- Salt and freshly ground black pepper to taste

For the Remoulade:
- ½ cup mayonnaise
- 1 tablespoon Dijon mustard
- 1 tablespoon ketchup
- 1 tablespoon chopped green onion
- 1 tablespoon chopped fresh parsley
- 1 teaspoon lemon juice
- ½ teaspoon hot sauce (adjust to your spice preference)
- Pinch of paprika
- Salt and freshly ground black pepper to taste

Instructions

1. Preheat your Breville Smart Air Fryer Oven Pro to 400°F (200°C) using the "Air Fry" function. Pat the mahi-mahi fillets dry with paper towels.
2. In a shallow bowl, combine olive oil, paprika, cayenne pepper, garlic powder, onion powder, salt, and pepper. Rub the spice mixture generously all over the mahi-mahi fillets, ensuring they are well coated.
3. **For the Remoulade**: In a small bowl, whisk together mayonnaise, Dijon mustard, ketchup, green onion, parsley, lemon juice, hot sauce, paprika, salt, and pepper.
4. Place the mahi-mahi fillets in a single layer in the air fryer basket, ensuring they don't touch.
5. Air fry for 10-12 minutes, or until the mahi-mahi fillets are cooked through and flake easily with a fork. The internal temperature should reach 145°F (63°C) for safe consumption.

Tips

- Mahi-mahi is a delicate fish, so be gentle when handling it.
- You can substitute cod or another firm white fish for mahi-mahi in this recipe.
- Adjust the amount of cayenne pepper in the spice mixture to suit your spice preference.
- Serve the air-fried Cajun mahi-mahi with the prepared remoulade sauce for dipping. You can also pair it with roasted vegetables, rice, or quinoa for a complete meal.

Nutritional Information (per serving)
Calories: 500, **Fat**: 30g, **Protein**: 45g, **Carbs**: 5g

This recipe brings the bold flavors of Cajun cuisine to your air fryer with succulent mahi-mahi fillets seasoned with a spicy blend.

SERVES	PREP TIME	COOK TIME
2	10 minutes	5 - 7 minutes

AIR-FRIED SCALLOPS WITH LEMON BUTTER SAUCE

Ingredients

- 1 pound large sea scallops
- 1 tablespoon olive oil
- Salt and freshly ground black pepper to taste
- 2 tablespoons butter
- 1 tablespoon lemon juice
- 1 teaspoon chopped fresh parsley (for garnish)

Instructions

1. Preheat your Breville Smart Air Fryer Oven Pro to 400°F (200°C) using the "Air Fry" function. Pat the sea scallops dry with paper towels.
2. Season the sea scallops generously with salt and pepper.
3. In a small saucepan, melt the butter over medium heat. Once melted, add the lemon juice and cook for a minute, swirling the pan occasionally, until slightly thickened.
4. Lightly coat the air fryer basket with cooking spray. Arrange the sea scallops in a single layer in the basket, ensuring they don't touch.
5. Air fry for 5-7 minutes, or until the scallops are golden brown and cooked through. They should be opaque throughout with a slight sear on the outside.
6. Remove the air fryer basket and immediately spoon the lemon butter sauce over the cooked scallops.

Tips

- Use dry sea scallops for optimal air frying results. Wet scallops may release excess moisture and prevent them from browning properly.
- Don't overcrowd the air fryer basket as it can affect even cooking.
- Be careful not to overcook the scallops, as they can become tough and rubbery.
- Serve the air-fried scallops with roasted asparagus, risotto, or mashed potatoes for a luxurious meal.
- Garnish with fresh chopped parsley for an extra touch of elegance.

Alex & Jamie
Blake

Nutritional Information (per serving)
Calories: 400, **Fat**: 30g,
Protein: 35g, **Carbs**: 5g

This recipe showcases the delicate sweetness of sea scallops cooked to perfection and drizzled with a simple yet flavorful lemon butter sauce.

SERVES
2 - 3

 PREP TIME
20 minutes

 COOK TIME
10 - 12 minutes

CRISPY CALAMARI WITH SPICY MARINARA SAUCE

Ingredients

- 1 pound calamari rings and tentacles, cleaned and patted dry
- ½ cup all-purpose flour
- 1 teaspoon paprika
- ½ teaspoon garlic powder
- ½ teaspoon onion powder
- Salt and freshly ground black pepper to taste
- 1 tablespoon olive oil

For the Spicy Marinara Sauce:

- 1 (14.5 oz) can diced tomatoes, undrained
- 1 tablespoon tomato paste
- ½ teaspoon dried oregano
- ¼ teaspoon red pepper flakes (adjust to your spice preference)
- 1 clove garlic, minced
- Salt and freshly ground black pepper to taste

Instructions

1. Preheat your Breville Smart Air Fryer Oven Pro to 400°F (200°C) using the "Air Fry" function.
2. In a shallow bowl, combine flour, paprika, garlic powder, onion powder, salt, and pepper. Dredge the calamari rings and tentacles in the seasoned flour mixture, ensuring they are evenly coated.
3. For the Spicy Marinara Sauce: In a saucepan, combine diced tomatoes, tomato paste, oregano, red pepper flakes, garlic, salt, and pepper. Bring to a simmer over medium heat and cook for 10 minutes, stirring occasionally, until slightly thickened. Taste and adjust seasonings as needed.
4. Lightly coat the air fryer basket with cooking spray. Arrange the breaded calamari pieces in a single layer, ensuring they don't touch.
5. Air fry for 10-12 minutes, or until the calamari is golden brown and crispy on the outside, and cooked through (no longer translucent) on the inside.

Tips

- To clean calamari, remove the head, tentacles, and internal organs. Pull out the clear cartilage (pen) running through the body. Rinse thoroughly under cold water and pat dry with paper towels. Cut the body into rings and tentacles into bite-sized pieces.
- Serve the air-fried calamari hot with the prepared spicy marinara sauce for dipping. You can also garnish with a lemon wedge and fresh parsley for added flavor and visual appeal.

Alex & Jamie
Blake

Nutritional Information
(per serving)
Calories: 500, **Fat**: 25g,
Protein: 40g, **Carbs**: 30g

This recipe transforms classic calamari into a healthier and crispier version using your Breville Smart Air Fryer Oven Pro

	SERVES		PREP TIME		COOK TIME
	2		20 minutes		10 - 12 minutes

AIR-FRIED FISH TACOS WITH CHIPOTLE CREMA

Ingredients

- 2 (4 oz) cod fillets or other white fish fillets
- ½ cup all-purpose flour
- 1 teaspoon chili powder
- ½ teaspoon smoked paprika
- ¼ teaspoon cumin
- Salt and freshly ground black pepper to taste
- 2 corn tortillas
- Toppings (optional): shredded cabbage, diced avocado, salsa, lime wedges

For the Chipotle Crema:
- ½ cup sour cream
- 1 tablespoon mayonnaise
- 1 chipotle pepper in adobo sauce, minced (adjust to your spice preference)
- 1 clove garlic, minced
- 1 tablespoon lime juice
- Salt and freshly ground black pepper to taste

Instructions

1. Preheat your Breville Smart Air Fryer Oven Pro to 400°F (200°C) using the "Air Fry" function. Pat the fish fillets dry with paper towels.
2. In a shallow bowl, combine flour, chili powder, paprika, cumin, salt, and pepper. Dredge the fish fillets in the seasoned flour mixture, ensuring they are evenly coated.
3. **For the Chipotle Crema**: In a small bowl, whisk together sour cream, mayonnaise, chipotle pepper in adobo sauce, garlic, lime juice, salt, and pepper.
4. Lightly coat the air fryer basket with cooking spray. Arrange the breaded fish fillets in a single layer, ensuring they don't touch.
5. Air fry for 10-12 minutes, or until the fish is cooked through and flakes easily with a fork. The internal temperature should reach 145°F (63°C) for safe consumption.

To Assemble Tacos:

6. Warm the corn tortillas in your Breville Smart Air Fryer Oven Pro using the "Bake" function for a few minutes (optional).
7. Place the cooked fish fillets on the warmed tortillas.
8. Add your desired toppings like shredded cabbage, diced avocado, salsa, and a squeeze of lime juice.
9. Drizzle with the prepared chipotle crema and enjoy!

Tips

- You can use any type of white fish that flakes easily, such as tilapia or haddock, for this recipe.
- Serve the air-fried fish tacos with a side of rice or black beans for a complete meal.

Nutritional Information
(per serving)
Calories: 500, **Fat**: 30g,
Protein: 40g, **Carbs**: 30g

This recipe brings the taste of Baja to your air fryer with flaky white fish tacos drizzled with a creamy chipotle crema.

SERVES 2   **PREP TIME** 20 minutes   **COOK TIME** 12 - 15 minutes

AIR-FRIED SALMON BURGERS WITH LEMON DILL SAUCE

Ingredients

- 1 pound salmon fillet, skin removed and chopped
- ¼ cup breadcrumbs
- 1 tablespoon chopped fresh dill
- 1 tablespoon olive oil
- Salt and freshly ground black pepper to taste
- Hamburger buns

For the Lemon Dill Sauce:
- ½ cup mayonnaise
- 1 tablespoon sour cream
- 1 tablespoon chopped fresh dill
- 1 tablespoon lemon juice
- Salt and freshly ground black pepper to taste
- Optional: Chopped red onion for garnish

Instructions

1. In a large bowl, combine chopped salmon, breadcrumbs, dill, olive oil, salt, and pepper. Mix well to combine and form two equal-sized patties.
2. Preheat your Breville Smart Air Fryer Oven Pro to 400°F (200°C) using the "Air Fry" function. Lightly coat the air fryer basket with cooking spray.
3. For the Lemon Dill Sauce: In a small bowl, whisk together mayonnaise, sour cream, dill, lemon juice, salt, and pepper. Add chopped red onion for a bit of extra flavor and crunch (optional).
4. Place the salmon burger patties in the air fryer basket, ensuring they don't touch.
5. Air fry for 12-15 minutes, or until the salmon burgers are cooked through and reach an internal temperature of 145°F (63°C). Flip the burgers halfway through cooking for even browning.
6. To Assemble Burgers:
7. Toast the hamburger buns in your air fryer using the "Bake" function for a few minutes (optional).
8. Place the cooked salmon burger on the bottom bun.
9. Top with your favorite burger toppings like lettuce, tomato, cheese, and red onion.
10. Drizzle with the prepared lemon dill sauce and enjoy!

Tips

- If the salmon mixture seems too loose, add a tablespoon of panko breadcrumbs or flaxseed meal for extra binding.
- You can also form the salmon mixture into smaller patties for sliders. Adjust the cooking time accordingly.
- Serve the air-fried salmon burgers with a side of sweet potato fries or a salad for a balanced meal.

Nutritional Information (per serving)

Calories: 500, **Fat**: 30g, **Protein**: 45g, **Carbs**: 30g

This recipe transforms salmon into juicy and flavorful burgers, perfect for a lighter and healthier take on classic hamburgers.

VEGETARIAN VIBES

UNLOCKING FLAVORFUL AIR-FRIED DELIGHTS WITH THE BREVILLE SMART AIR FRYER OVEN PRO

Embark on a culinary adventure through the world of plant-based cuisine with this chapter dedicated to ten vibrant vegetarian recipes. Utilizing the Breville Smart Air Fryer Oven Pro, we'll explore air-fried creations that are not only delicious but also convenient and healthy. From protein-packed tofu scrambles to hearty lentil shepherd's pie, these recipes cater to a variety of dietary needs while showcasing the versatility of air frying for vegetarians.

Alex & Jamie
Blake

Alex & Jamie Blake

| SERVES 2 | PREP TIME 10 minutes | COOK TIME 10 - 12 minutes |

AIR-FRIED SPICY TOFU SCRAMBLE

Ingredients

- 1 (14 oz) block firm tofu, drained and pressed
- ½ cup chopped vegetables (bell pepper, onion, mushrooms, etc.)
- ¼ cup crumbled tempeh (optional)
- 1 tablespoon olive oil
- ½ teaspoon turmeric powder
- ¼ teaspoon cumin
- ¼ teaspoon smoked paprika
- Pinch of cayenne pepper (adjust to your spice preference)
- Salt and freshly ground black pepper to taste
- ¼ cup chopped fresh parsley (for garnish)

Instructions

1. Preheat your Breville Smart Air Fryer Oven Pro to 400°F (200°C) using the "Air Fry" function.
2. Crumble the tofu with your hands or a fork into bite-sized pieces.
3. In a large bowl, combine crumbled tofu, chopped vegetables, and tempeh (if using).
4. Drizzle with olive oil and toss with turmeric powder, cumin, paprika, cayenne pepper, salt, and pepper. Ensure all ingredients are evenly coated.
5. Lightly coat the air fryer basket with cooking spray. Spread the tofu scramble mixture in a single layer in the basket.
6. Air fry for 10-12 minutes, or until the tofu is golden brown and slightly crispy on the edges. Stir the mixture occasionally for even cooking.

Tips

- To press the tofu, wrap it in a clean kitchen towel and place a heavy object on top for at least 15 minutes. This removes excess moisture for a better browning effect.
- You can substitute tempeh for crumbled cooked sausage or chorizo for a different flavor profile.
- Serve the air-fried tofu scramble with your favorite breakfast toppings like avocado slices, chopped tomatoes, salsa, or vegan cheese. Garnish with fresh parsley for an extra pop of color and freshness.

Nutritional Information (per serving)

Calories: 350, **Fat**: 15g, **Protein**: 25g, **Carbs**: 20g

This recipe transforms tofu into a flavorful and satisfying breakfast scramble, perfect for a protein-rich and veggie-packed start to your day.

SERVES
2

 PREP TIME
20 minutes

 COOK TIME
15 - 20 minutes

PORTOBELLO BURGERS WITH BALSAMIC GLAZE

Ingredients

- 2 large portobello mushroom caps, stems removed
- 1 cup cooked brown rice
- ½ cup black beans, drained and rinsed
- ¼ cup chopped red onion
- 2 tablespoons chopped fresh parsley
- 1 tablespoon olive oil
- 1 tablespoon balsamic vinegar
- 1 teaspoon soy sauce
- ½ teaspoon dried oregano
- Salt and freshly ground black pepper to taste
- Hamburger buns

For the Balsamic Glaze (Optional):
- ½ cup balsamic vinegar
- 1 tablespoon brown sugar

Instructions

1. Preheat your Breville Smart Air Fryer Oven Pro to 400°F (200°C) using the "Air Fry" function.
2. In a large bowl, combine cooked brown rice, black beans, red onion, parsley, olive oil, balsamic vinegar, soy sauce, oregano, salt, and pepper. Mix well to combine and form two equal-sized patties.
3. Gently brush the tops of the portobello mushroom caps with olive oil.
4. Place the portobello mushroom caps gill-side down in a baking dish. Bake in a preheated oven at 400°F (200°C) for 5-7 minutes to soften them slightly.

For the Balsamic Glaze (Optional):
- In a small saucepan, combine balsamic vinegar and brown sugar. Bring to a simmer over medium heat and cook for 10-15 minutes, or until the mixture thickens and reduces by half.

To Assemble Burgers:
5. Remove the portobello mushroom caps from the oven and carefully fill each cap with a prepared brown rice and black bean patty.
6. Place the stuffed portobello mushrooms in the air fryer basket, gill-side up.
7. Air fry for 10-12 minutes, or until the burger patties are heated through and the portobello mushrooms are tender.
8. During the last few minutes of cooking, you can brush the tops of the burgers with balsamic glaze for a sweet and tangy flavor (optional).

Alex & Jamie
Blake

Nutritional Information (per serving)
Calories: 500, **Fat**: 20g,
Protein: 25g, **Carbs**: 50g

This recipe transforms portobello mushrooms into hearty and flavorful burger patties, perfect for a satisfying vegetarian main course.

SERVES
2 - 3

PREP TIME
10 minutes

 COOK TIME
12 - 15 minutes

AIR-FRIED VEGGIE FAJITAS

Alex & Jamie
Blake

Ingredients

- bell pepper (any color), sliced
- 1 red onion, sliced
- 1 cup broccoli florets
- ½ cup sliced mushrooms
- 1 tablespoon olive oil
- 1 teaspoon chili powder
- ½ teaspoon cumin
- ¼ teaspoon smoked paprika
- Salt and freshly ground black pepper to taste
- 2-3 fajita tortillas (warmed)

For the toppings (optional):
- Guacamole
- Salsa
- Sour cream
- Vegan cheese
- Chopped fresh cilantro

Instructions

1. Preheat your Breville Smart Air Fryer Oven Pro to 400°F (200°C) using the "Air Fry" function.
2. In a large bowl, combine sliced bell pepper, onion, broccoli florets, and mushrooms.
3. Drizzle with olive oil and toss with chili powder, cumin, paprika, salt, and pepper. Ensure all ingredients are evenly coated.
4. Lightly coat the air fryer basket with cooking spray. Spread the veggie mixture in a single layer in the basket, ensuring the pieces don't touch.
5. Air fry for 12-15 minutes, or until the vegetables are tender-crisp and slightly browned. Stir the mixture occasionally for even cooking.

To Assemble Fajitas:
6. Warm the fajita tortillas according to package instructions or using the "Bake" function on your air fryer.
7. Fill each warmed tortilla with your desired amount of air-fried veggies.
8. Add your favorite toppings like guacamole, salsa, sour cream, vegan cheese, and chopped fresh cilantro.

Tips

- You can add other vegetables to this recipe, such as zucchini, yellow squash, or poblano peppers.
- Serve the air-fried veggie fajitas with a side of brown rice or quinoa for a complete meal.
- For a smoky flavor, you can add a teaspoon of smoked paprika to the spice mixture

Nutritional Information (per serving)
Calories: 350, **Fat**: 10g,
Protein: 5g, **Carbs**: 50g

This recipe offers a quick and flavorful vegetarian take on fajitas, featuring a variety of air-fried vegetables .

SERVES
4

 PREP TIME
20 minutes

 COOK TIME
40 - 45 minutes

LENTIL SHEPHERD'S PIE

Ingredients

- 1 cup brown lentils, rinsed
- 2 cups vegetable broth
- 1 tablespoon olive oil
- 1 onion, chopped
- 2 carrots, chopped
- 2 celery stalks, chopped
- 2 cloves garlic, minced
- 1 cup frozen peas
- 1 tablespoon tomato paste
- 1 teaspoon dried thyme
- ½ teaspoon dried rosemary
- Salt and freshly ground black pepper to taste

For the Mashed Potatoes:
- 2 pounds russet potatoes, peeled and cubed
- ½ cup unsweetened plant-based milk
- 2 tablespoons vegan butter
- Salt and freshly ground black pepper to taste

Instructions

1. In a medium saucepan, combine rinsed lentils and vegetable broth. Bring to a boil, then reduce heat, cover, and simmer for 20-25 minutes, or until lentils are tender.
2. Preheat your Breville Smart Air Fryer Oven Pro to 400°F (200°C) using the "Air Fry" function.
3. While the lentils cook, heat olive oil in a large skillet over medium heat. Add chopped onion, carrots, and celery. Sauté for 5-7 minutes, or until softened.
4. Add minced garlic and cook for an additional minute, until fragrant.
5. Stir in frozen peas, tomato paste, dried thyme, and dried rosemary. Cook for another minute, allowing the flavors to meld.
6. Once the lentils are cooked, drain any excess liquid and add them to the vegetable mixture in the skillet. Season with salt and freshly ground black pepper to taste.

Preparing the Mashed Potatoes:
7. While the lentil mixture simmers, bring a large pot of salted water to a boil. Add cubed potatoes and cook for 15-20 minutes, or until fork-tender.
8. Drain the cooked potatoes and return them to the pot.
9. Using a potato masher or hand mixer, mash the potatoes until smooth. Gradually add unsweetened plant-based milk and vegan butter while mashing until you reach a desired creamy consistency. Season with salt and freshly ground black pepper to taste.

Assembling the Shepherd's Pie:
10. Preheat a baking dish (approximately 2-quart size) in your oven at 400°F (200°C) for a few minutes.
11. Spoon the cooked lentil and vegetable mixture into the preheated baking dish. Spread it evenly.
12. Top the lentil mixture with the prepared mashed potatoes, creating a smooth and even layer.
13. Place the baking dish in the air fryer basket (ensure the preheating is complete).
14. Air fry for 10-12 minutes, or until the mashed potato topping is golden brown and slightly crispy on the edges.

Alex & Jamie
Blake

Nutritional Information
(per serving)
Calories: 500, **Fat**: 15g,
Protein: 20g, **Carbs**: 60g

This recipe offers a hearty and comforting vegetarian twist on the classic shepherd's pie.

SERVES
2 - 3

 PREP TIME
15 minutes

 COOK TIME
20 - 25 minutes

BUFFALO CAULIFLOWER WINGS

Ingredients

- 1 head cauliflower, cut into florets
- ½ cup all-purpose flour
- 1 teaspoon paprika
- ½ teaspoon garlic powder
- ½ teaspoon onion powder
- Salt and freshly ground black pepper to taste
- 1 cup unsweetened plant-based milk
- ¼ cup hot sauce (adjust to your spice preference)
- 1 tablespoon melted vegan butter
- 1 tablespoon olive oil

Instructions

1. Preheat your Breville Smart Air Fryer Oven Pro to 400°F (200°C) using the "Air Fry" function.
2. In a large bowl, combine flour, paprika, garlic powder, onion powder, salt, and pepper. Toss the cauliflower florets in the dry mixture to coat them evenly.
3. In a separate bowl, whisk together plant-based milk, hot sauce, melted vegan butter, and olive oil. This will create your buffalo sauce.
4. Lightly coat the air fryer basket with cooking spray. Arrange the breaded cauliflower florets in a single layer in the basket, ensuring they don't touch.
5. Air fry for 15-20 minutes, or until the cauliflower florets are tender-crisp and golden brown. Shake the basket occasionally for even cooking.
6. Once cooked, remove the cauliflower florets from the air fryer and toss them in the prepared buffalo sauce until they are well coated.

Tips

- For extra crispy cauliflower wings, double coat them. After coating the florets in the dry mixture, dip them in the wet buffalo sauce mixture before coating them again with the dry mixture.
- You can adjust the level of spice by using a milder or hotter hot sauce.
- Serve the air-fried buffalo cauliflower wings with your favorite dipping sauces like vegan ranch dressing or blue cheese dressing. Celery sticks and carrot sticks also make great accompaniments.

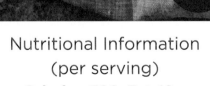

Nutritional Information
(per serving)
Calories: 300, **Fat**: 10g,
Protein: 5g, **Carbs**: 35g

Spice up your Breville Smart Air Fryer Oven Pro with these crispy and flavorful buffalo cauliflower wings, perfect for a game night or satisfying snack.

SERVES	PREP TIME	COOK TIME
2 - 3	20 minutes	10 - 12 minutes

VEGGIE SPRING ROLLS

Ingredients

- 10 rice paper wrappers
- 1 cup shredded carrots
- 1 cup shredded red cabbage
- ½ cup chopped cucumber
- ½ cup chopped bell pepper (any color)
- ¼ cup chopped fresh cilantro
- 1 cup cooked brown rice (optional)
- 1 tablespoon sesame oil
- 1 tablespoon soy sauce
- 1 tablespoon rice vinegar
- 1 teaspoon sriracha (optional)
- Salt and freshly ground black pepper to taste

Instructions

1. Prepare a shallow dish filled with warm water. This will be used to soften the rice paper wrappers.
2. In a large bowl, combine shredded carrots, red cabbage, cucumber, bell pepper, and fresh cilantro.
3. (Optional) If using cooked brown rice, add it to the vegetable mixture and toss to combine.
4. In a small bowl, whisk together sesame oil, soy sauce, rice vinegar, and sriracha (if using). Season with salt and freshly ground black pepper to taste.
5. Dip a single rice paper wrapper into the warm water for a few seconds, just until it becomes pliable. Lay it flat on a work surface.
6. Place a small amount of the vegetable mixture in the center of the softened rice paper wrapper. Drizzle with a little bit of the prepared sauce.
7. Fold the bottom of the rice paper wrapper over the filling, then fold in the sides. Tightly roll up the rice paper to create a spring roll. Repeat with the remaining rice paper wrappers and filling.
8. Preheat your Breville Smart Air Fryer Oven Pro to 400°F (200°C) using the "Air Fry" function. Lightly coat the air fryer basket with cooking spray.
9. Arrange the spring rolls in a single layer in the basket, ensuring they don't touch.
10. Air fry for 10-12 minutes, or until the spring rolls are golden brown and crispy. Flip them halfway through cooking for even browning.

Nutritional Information
(per serving)
Calories: 350, **Fat**: 5g,
Protein: 10g, **Carbs**: 55g

These air-fried spring rolls offer a healthier and lighter alternative to traditional fried spring rolls, featuring a variety of colorful vegetables.

SERVES 2 **PREP TIME** 10 minutes **COOK TIME** 5 - 7 minutes

BLACK BEAN AND CORN QUESADILLAS

Ingredients

- 2 large flour tortillas
- 1 cup cooked black beans, mashed slightly
- ½ cup frozen corn, thawed
- ¼ cup chopped red onion
- 1 tablespoon chopped fresh cilantro
- 1 jalapeño pepper, seeded and finely chopped (optional)
- 1 clove garlic, minced
- ½ cup shredded vegan cheese (optional)
- Salt and freshly ground black pepper to taste
- Olive oil spray

Instructions

1. Preheat your Breville Smart Air Fryer Oven Pro to 400°F (200°C) using the "Air Fry" function.
2. In a medium bowl, combine mashed black beans, thawed corn, chopped red onion, cilantro, jalapeño pepper (if using), minced garlic, and vegan cheese (if using). Season with salt and freshly ground black pepper to taste.
3. Place one flour tortilla on a work surface. Spread half of the black bean and corn filling evenly over one half of the tortilla.
4. Fold the tortilla in half, enclosing the filling. Lightly coat the outside of the folded tortilla with olive oil spray.
5. Repeat steps 3 and 4 to prepare the second quesadilla.
6. Place the prepared quesadillas in the air fryer basket, ensuring they don't touch.
7. Air fry for 5-7 minutes per quesadilla, or until the tortilla is golden brown and crispy, and the cheese is melted (if using). Flip the quesadilla halfway through cooking for even browning.

Tips

- You can use whole wheat tortillas for a more nutritious option.
- To add a smoky flavor, add a teaspoon of smoked paprika to the black bean and corn filling.
- Serve the air-fried black bean and corn quesadillas with your favorite toppings like salsa, guacamole, sour cream (for non-vegans), or vegan sour cream.

Nutritional Information (per serving)
Calories: 400, **Fat**: 15g, **Protein**: 15g, **Carbs**: 45g

These air-fried quesadillas offer a quick and satisfying vegetarian meal or snack.

	SERVES 2 - 3		PREP TIME 15 minutes		COOK TIME 10 - 12 minutes

HALLOUMI AND VEGETABLE SKEWERS

Ingredients

- 1 block halloumi cheese, cut into 1-inch cubes
- 1 bell pepper (any color), cut into squares
- 1 red onion, cut into wedges
- 1 zucchini, cut into thick slices
- 1 tablespoon olive oil
- 1 teaspoon dried oregano
- ½ teaspoon garlic powder
- Salt and freshly ground black pepper to taste
- Wooden skewers

Instructions

1. Preheat your Breville Smart Air Fryer Oven Pro to 400°F (200°C) using the "Air Fry" function.
2. In a large bowl, combine olive oil, dried oregano, garlic powder, salt, and pepper. Toss the cubed halloumi cheese, bell pepper squares, red onion wedges, and zucchini slices in the marinade to coat them evenly.
3. Thread the marinated vegetables and halloumi cheese cubes onto wooden skewers, alternating the ingredients for a visually appealing presentation.
4. Lightly coat the air fryer basket with cooking spray. Place the skewers in the basket, ensuring they don't touch.
5. Air fry for 10-12 minutes, or until the vegetables are tender-crisp and the halloumi cheese is golden brown on all sides. Flip the skewers halfway through cooking for even browning.

Tips

- Soak wooden skewers in water for at least 30 minutes before threading to prevent them from burning during air frying.
- You can add other vegetables to this recipe, such as cherry tomatoes, mushrooms, or eggplant.
- Serve the air-fried halloumi and vegetable skewers with your favorite dipping sauces like tzatziki sauce, hummus, or a simple lemon vinaigrette.
- If you don't have halloumi cheese, you can substitute it with paneer cheese or firm tofu that has been marinated and cubed.

Nutritional Information (per serving)
Calories: 400, **Fat**: 20g,
Protein: 20g, **Carbs**: 25g

This recipe offers a colorful and flavorful vegetarian kabob option.

	SERVES		PREP TIME		COOK TIME
	2 - 3		15 minutes		20 - 25 minutes

ALOO GOBI (INDIAN SPICED POTATO & CAULIFLOWER)

Alex & Jamie
Blake

Ingredients

- 1 medium cauliflower, cut into florets
- 2 medium potatoes, peeled and cut into cubes
- 1 tablespoon olive oil
- 1 teaspoon cumin seeds
- ½ teaspoon turmeric powder
- ½ teaspoon coriander powder
- ¼ teaspoon chili powder (adjust to your spice preference)
- Salt and freshly ground black pepper to taste
- Chopped fresh cilantro (for garnish)

Instructions

1. Preheat your Breville Smart Air Fryer Oven Pro to 400°F (200°C) using the "Air Fry" function.
2. In a large bowl, combine cauliflower florets and potato cubes. Toss them with olive oil to coat evenly.
3. In a small bowl, mix together cumin seeds, turmeric powder, coriander powder, chili powder, salt, and pepper.
4. Sprinkle the spice mixture over the cauliflower and potato mixture in the large bowl. Toss well to ensure all ingredients are evenly coated.
5. Lightly coat the air fryer basket with cooking spray. Spread the cauliflower and potato mixture in a single layer in the basket, ensuring they don't touch.
6. Air fry for 20-25 minutes, or until the cauliflower florets are tender-crisp and the potatoes are golden brown and cooked through. Stir the mixture occasionally for even cooking.

Tips

- You can add other vegetables to this recipe, such as green beans, carrots, or peas.
- For a richer flavor, add a tablespoon of chopped cashews or peanuts to the spice mixture.
- Serve the air-fried aloo gobi hot, garnished with chopped fresh cilantro, and enjoy it with rice or naan bread.

Nutritional Information
(per serving)
Calories: 300, **Fat**: 10g,
Protein: 5g, **Carbs**: 40g

This recipe features air-fried cauliflower and potatoes tossed in a flavorful blend of Indian spices.

VEGGIE BURGERS WITH SWEET POTATO FRIES

Ingredients

For the Veggie Burgers:
- 1 can (15 oz) black beans, rinsed and drained
- 1 cup cooked quinoa
- ½ cup grated carrot
- ¼ cup chopped red onion
- 2 tablespoons chopped fresh parsley
- 1 tablespoon olive oil
- 1 teaspoon ground cumin
- ½ teaspoon chili powder
- Salt and freshly ground black pepper to taste
- Hamburger buns

For the Sweet Potato Fries:
- 1 medium sweet potato, cut into wedges
- 1 tablespoon olive oil
- ½ teaspoon smoked paprika
- Salt and freshly ground black pepper to taste

Instructions

For the Veggie Burgers:
1. In a large bowl, mash the black beans with a fork, leaving some texture.
2. Add cooked quinoa, grated carrot, chopped red onion, chopped parsley, olive oil, ground cumin, chili powder, salt, and pepper. Mix well to combine and form two equal-sized patties.

For the Sweet Potato Fries:
3. Preheat your Breville Smart Air Fryer Oven Pro to 400°F (200°C) using the "Air Fry" function.
4. In a medium bowl, toss sweet potato wedges with olive oil, smoked paprika, salt, and pepper.

Cooking and Assembly:
5. Lightly coat the air fryer basket with cooking spray. Place the veggie burger patties in the basket, ensuring they don't touch.
6. Arrange the sweet potato wedges in a separate layer in the basket (use a second basket or cook them in batches if needed).
7. Air fry for 15-20 minutes, or until the veggie burger patties are cooked through and the sweet potato fries are golden brown and tender-crisp. Flip the burger patties and fries halfway through cooking for even browning.

Tips

- To bind the veggie burger patties better, you can add a tablespoon of flaxseed meal mixed with 3 tablespoons of water and let it sit for 5 minutes before adding it to the mixture.

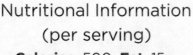

Nutritional Information (per serving)
Calories: 500, **Fat**: 15g, **Protein**: 20g, **Carbs**: 60g

This recipe offers a vegetarian burger option featuring air-fried veggie patties.

BREAD, PIZZA & PANINI POWER

10 RECIPES UTILIZING BREVILLE SMART AIR FRYER OVEN PRO FUNCTIONS

This chapter unlocks the potential of your Breville Smart Air Fryer Oven Pro for creating bakery-worthy breads, gourmet pizzas, cheesy paninis, and decadent calzones. We'll utilize various functions like Bake, Bagel, Toast, and Pizza to achieve crispy crusts, fluffy interiors, and perfectly melted cheese. Get ready to transform your air fryer into a bread-making powerhouse!

	SERVES		PREP TIME		COOK TIME
	4 - 6		10 minutes		20 minutes

AIR-FRIED CRUSTY BAGUETTES

Ingredients

- 3 cups all-purpose flour, plus extra for dusting
- 1 1/2 teaspoons active dry yeast
- 1 1/2 teaspoons salt
- 1 1/4 cups warm water (105°F)

Instructions

1. In a large bowl, combine flour, yeast, and salt.
2. Slowly add warm water to the dry ingredients, mixing with a wooden spoon until a shaggy dough forms.
3. Transfer the dough to a lightly floured surface and knead for 10 minutes until smooth and elastic.
4. Place the dough in a greased bowl, cover with plastic wrap, and let rise in a warm place for 1 hour, or until doubled in size.
5. Preheat your Breville Smart Air Fryer Oven Pro to 400°F (200°C) using the "Bake" function.
6. Punch down the dough and divide it in half. Shape each half into a long baguette, about 12 inches long. Dust the baguettes with flour and place them on a baking sheet lined with parchment paper.
7. Using a sharp knife, make diagonal slashes on the top of each baguette.
8. Bake the baguettes for 20 minutes, or until golden brown and crusty.
9. Remove from the oven and let cool on a wire rack for at least 15 minutes before slicing and serving.

Tips

- For a chewier crust, preheat a baking sheet in the oven while the baguettes rise. Carefully transfer the shaped baguettes to the preheated baking sheet before baking.
- You can brush the baguettes with olive oil before baking for a richer flavor.

Nutritional Information (per serving)
Calories: 220, **Fat**: 2g,
Protein: 8g, **Carbs**: 42g

These baguettes boast a crisp exterior and a chewy interior, perfect for dipping in olive oil and balsamic vinegar.

| SERVES 4 - 6 | PREP TIME 20 minutes | COOK TIME 20 - 25 minutes |

DEEP-DISH VEGGIE PIZZA

Alex & Jamie
Blake

Ingredients

For the Crust:
- 1 1/2 cups all-purpose flour
- 1/2 teaspoon salt
- 1/2 cup cold unsalted butter, cubed
- 3 tablespoons ice water

For the Toppings:
- 1/2 cup pizza sauce
- 1 cup shredded mozzarella cheese
- 1/2 cup chopped red onion
- 1/2 cup sliced green bell pepper
- 1/2 cup sliced mushrooms
- 1/4 cup chopped black olives
- Pinch of dried oregano
- Pinch of red pepper flakes (optional)

Instructions

1. In a food processor, combine flour and salt. Pulse a few times to combine.
2. Add the cold butter cubes and pulse until the mixture resembles coarse crumbs.
3. With the motor running, slowly add the ice water through the feed tube until the dough just comes together. Be careful not to overmix.
4. Press the dough into a greased 8-inch round cake pan. Gently push the dough up the sides to form a crust. Freeze the crust for 15 minutes.
5. Preheat your Breville Smart Air Fryer Oven Pro to 400°F (200°C) using the "Pizza" function.
6. Spread pizza sauce over the chilled crust. Top with mozzarella cheese, red onion, green pepper, mushrooms, black olives, oregano, and red pepper flakes (if using).
7. Bake for 20-25 minutes, or until the crust is golden brown and the cheese is melted and bubbly.
8. Let the pizza cool slightly before slicing and serving.

Tips

- You can customize this recipe with your favorite vegetables. Some other options include artichoke hearts, roasted zucchini, or sun-dried tomatoes.
- Pre-cook vegetables with a bit of olive oil in the air fryer for 5 minutes before adding them to the pizza for a softer texture.

Nutritional Information
(per serving)
Calories: 500, **Fat**: 25g,
Protein: 20g, **Carbs**: 55g

This recipe offers a delicious twist on traditional pizza with a thick, flavorful crust and a variety of fresh vegetables.

CHEESY HAM AND SWISS PANINI

Ingredients

- 2 slices sourdough bread
- 2 tablespoons butter, softened
- 2 slices deli ham
- 2 slices Swiss cheese
- 1 tablespoon Dijon mustard

Instructions

1. Preheat your Breville Smart Air Fryer Oven Pro to 400°F (200°C) using the "Toast" function.
2. Spread the softened butter on one side of each bread slice.
3. Spread Dijon mustard on the other side of one bread slice.
4. Layer the ham and Swiss cheese on the mustard-coated bread slice.
5. Top with the other bread slice, buttered side facing out.
6. Place the panini on a baking sheet or the air fryer basket.
7. Toast for 5-7 minutes, or until golden brown and the cheese is melted and gooey.
8. Flip the panini halfway through cooking for even browning.

Tips

- You can use any type of bread you like for paninis, such as ciabatta, focaccia, or wheat bread.
- Get creative with your fillings! Other delicious options include roasted vegetables, pesto and mozzarella, or grilled chicken with avocado.

Alex & Jamie
Blake

Nutritional Information
(per serving)
Calories: 450, **Fat**: 25g,
Protein: 20g, **Carbs**: 40g

This classic panini recipe is a quick and satisfying lunch option.

64

SERVES 2 - 3		PREP TIME 15 minutes		COOK TIME 15 - 20 minutes	

DECADENT CALZONES

Ingredients

- 1 cup pizza dough (store-bought or homemade)
- 1/4 cup ricotta cheese
- 1/2 cup shredded mozzarella cheese
- 1/4 cup chopped pepperoni
- 1/4 cup chopped marinara sauce
- 1 tablespoon chopped fresh parsley

Instructions

1. Preheat your Breville Smart Air Fryer Oven Pro to 400°F (200°C) using the "Bake" function.
2. Divide the pizza dough into two equal pieces. Roll each piece out into a thin circle.
3. Spread ricotta cheese in the center of each dough circle. Top with mozzarella cheese, pepperoni, and marinara sauce.
4. Fold the dough circles in half, forming crescents. Pinch the edges to seal.
5. Brush the calzones with olive oil and sprinkle with a pinch of salt.
6. Place the calzones on a baking sheet lined with parchment paper.
7. Bake for 15-20 minutes, or until golden brown and the filling is heated through.
8. Let cool slightly before serving. Garnish with fresh parsley.

Tips

- You can add other toppings to your calzones, such as sausage, mushrooms, or roasted vegetables.
- For a cheesier calzone, brush the inside of the dough circle with melted butter before adding the fillings.

Nutritional Information (per serving)

Calories: 500, **Fat**: 20g,
Protein: 25g, **Carbs**: 50g

These air-fried calzones offer a lighter alternative to deep-fried versions, filled with ricotta cheese, mozzarella, and your favorite pizza toppings.

SPEEDY PESTO PINWHEELS

Ingredients

- 1 sheet frozen puff pastry, thawed
- 1/4 cup prepared pesto
- 1/4 cup shredded mozzarella cheese
- 1/4 cup sun-dried tomatoes, chopped (optional)
- Pinch of dried oregano
- Fresh cracked black pepper (optional)

Instructions

1. Preheat your Breville Smart Air Fryer Oven Pro to 400°F (200°C) using the "Bake" function. Lightly grease a baking sheet or the air fryer basket.
2. Unfold the puff pastry sheet and spread a thin layer of pesto evenly over the entire surface.
3. Sprinkle the mozzarella cheese on top of the pesto, followed by the chopped sun-dried tomatoes (if using).
4. Season with a pinch of dried oregano and black pepper (optional).
5. Starting from a long edge, roll the puff pastry sheet tightly into a log.
6. Using a sharp knife, slice the log into 1-inch thick pinwheels.
7. Arrange the pinwheels on the prepared baking sheet or air fryer basket, leaving space between them for even cooking.
8. Bake for 10-12 minutes, or until the puff pastry is golden brown and flaky and the cheese is melted and bubbly.
9. Let cool slightly before serving.

Tips

- You can substitute the pesto with another spread of your choice, such as ricotta cheese mixed with chopped herbs or marinara sauce.
- Add a touch of crumbled cooked sausage or chicken for a more filling option.
- Brush the pinwheels with a beaten egg wash before baking for an extra glossy sheen.
- Leftover pinwheels can be stored in an airtight container at room temperature for up to 2 days. Reheat them in the air fryer for a few minutes to crisp them back up.

Alex & Jamie
Blake

Nutritional Information (per serving)

Calories: 350, **Fat**: 20g,
Protein: 10g, **Carbs**: 35g

These flavorful pesto pinwheels are a breeze to prepare and offer a delightful twist on the classic pinwheel appetizer.

SERVES	PREP TIME	COOK TIME
4 - 6	10 minutes	20 -25 minutes

MINI HERB AND CHEESE FOCACCIA

Ingredients

- 1 1/2 cups all-purpose flour
- 1 teaspoon active dry yeast
- 1 teaspoon sugar
- 1/2 teaspoon salt
- 1/2 cup warm water (105°F)
- 2 tablespoons olive oil
- 2 tablespoons chopped fresh rosemary
- 2 tablespoons chopped fresh thyme
- Flaky sea salt (for sprinkling)

Instructions

1. In a large bowl, combine flour, yeast, sugar, and salt.
2. Add the warm water and olive oil to the dry ingredients. Mix with a wooden spoon until a shaggy dough forms.
3. Turn the dough onto a lightly floured surface and knead for 5 minutes until smooth and elastic.
4. Place the dough in a greased bowl, cover with plastic wrap, and let rise in a warm place for 1 hour, or until doubled in size.
5. Preheat your Breville Smart Air Fryer Oven Pro to 400°F (200°C) using the "Bake" function.
6. Grease a small baking pan or pie dish. Punch down the dough and transfer it to the prepared pan.
7. Using your fingertips, dimple the dough all over, creating indentations. Drizzle with additional olive oil and sprinkle with rosemary, thyme, and flaky sea salt.
8. Bake for 20-25 minutes, or until golden brown and cooked through.
9. Let cool slightly before slicing and serving.

Tips

- You can add other herbs to the focaccia, such as oregano or basil.
- For a richer flavor, add a grated clove of garlic to the olive oil before drizzling it on the dough.

Nutritional Information (per serving)

Calories: 300, **Fat**: 12g,
Protein: 6g, **Carbs**: 35g

This air-fried focaccia is perfect for a light lunch or appetizer.

SERVES	PREP TIME	COOK TIME
4	15 minutes	15 - 20 minutes

CRISPY EVERYTHING BAGELS

Ingredients

- 1 1/2 cups all-purpose flour, plus extra for dusting
- 1 teaspoon active dry yeast
- 1 tablespoon sugar
- 1 1/2 teaspoons salt
- 1 cup warm water (105°F)
- 1 tablespoon olive oil
- 1 egg white, beaten
- Everything bagel seasoning (for sprinkling)

Instructions

1. In a large bowl, combine flour, yeast, sugar, and salt.
2. Add the warm water and olive oil to the dry ingredients. Mix with a wooden spoon until a shaggy dough forms.
3. Turn the dough onto a lightly floured surface and knead for 10 minutes until smooth and elastic.
4. Place the dough in a greased bowl, cover with plastic wrap, and let rise in a warm place for 1 hour, or until doubled in size.
5. Preheat your Breville Smart Air Fryer Oven Pro to 400°F (200°C) using the "Bagel" function (if available) or "Bake" function.
6. Line a baking sheet with parchment paper. Divide the dough into 4 equal pieces. Shape each piece into a ball, then poke a hole in the center of each ball, widening the hole to form a bagel shape.
7. Cover the bagels with plastic wrap and let them rise for another 30 minutes.
8. In a small bowl, whisk the egg white with a tablespoon of water. Brush the bagels with the egg wash and sprinkle generously with everything bagel seasoning.
9. Place the bagels on the prepared baking sheet, leaving space between them.
10. Bake for 15-20 minutes, or until golden brown and cooked through.
11. Let the bagels cool slightly before slicing and serving.

Tips

- You can substitute the everything bagel seasoning with your favorite bagel toppings, such as sesame seeds, poppy seeds, or dried onion flakes.

Nutritional Information (per serving)

Calories: 250, **Fat**: 5g, **Protein**: 8g, **Carbs**: 40g

These air-fried bagels are a healthier alternative to traditional bagels, with a perfectly crispy exterior and a chewy interior.

SERVES
6

 PREP TIME
20 minutes

 COOK TIME
20 - 25 minutes

MINI QUICHES

Ingredients

For the Crust:
- 1 cup all-purpose flour
- 1/4 teaspoon salt
- 1/2 cup cold unsalted butter, cubed
- 3 tablespoons ice water

For the Filling:
- 4 eggs
- 1/2 cup milk
- 1/4 cup shredded cheddar cheese
- 1/4 cup chopped cooked ham
- 1/4 cup chopped cooked broccoli
- 1/4 teaspoon dried oregano
- Salt and pepper to taste

Instructions

1. In a food processor, combine flour and salt. Pulse a few times to combine.
2. Add the cold butter cubes and pulse until the mixture resembles coarse crumbs.
3. With the motor running, slowly add the ice water through the feed tube until the dough just comes together. Be careful not to overmix.
4. Press the dough into a greased muffin tin, forming small tart shells. Freeze the crusts for 15 minutes.
5. Preheat your Breville Smart Air Fryer Oven Pro to 375°F (190°C) using the "Bake" function.
6. In a large bowl, whisk together eggs, milk, cheddar cheese, ham, broccoli, oregano, salt, and pepper.
7. Pour the egg mixture into the prepared crusts.
8. Bake for 20-25 minutes, or until the quiches are set and the crusts are golden brown.
9. Let cool slightly before serving.

Tips

- You can customize the filling of your quiches with your favorite ingredients. Some other options include sausage, spinach, or mushrooms.
- Pre-cook any vegetables you're using in the filling to ensure they are tender in the final dish.

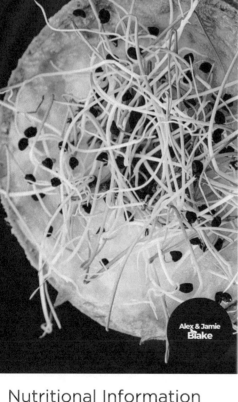

Alex & Jamie
Blake

Nutritional Information
(per serving)
Calories: 300, **Fat**: 18g,
Protein: 12g, **Carbs**: 20g

These individual quiches are perfect for a quick and easy breakfast or brunch.

69

SPICY BUFFALO CHICKEN CALZONES

Ingredients

- 1 cup pizza dough (store-bought or homemade)
- 1/2 cup cooked and shredded chicken breast
- 1/4 cup shredded mozzarella cheese
- 1/4 cup crumbled blue cheese
- 1/4 cup buffalo sauce
- 1 tablespoon chopped red onion
- Chopped celery (optional)

Instructions

1. Preheat your Breville Smart Air Fryer Oven Pro to 400°F (200°C) using the "Bake" function.
2. Divide the pizza dough into two equal pieces. Roll each piece out into a thin circle.
3. In a small bowl, combine cooked and shredded chicken breast, mozzarella cheese, blue cheese, buffalo sauce, and red onion. If using, add chopped celery for extra crunch.
4. Spread the buffalo chicken mixture evenly over one half of each dough circle. Leave a one-inch border around the edge.
5. Fold the dough circles in half, forming crescents. Pinch the edges to seal tightly, using a fork to crimp the edges if desired.
6. Brush the calzones with olive oil and sprinkle with a pinch of salt.
7. Place the calzones on a baking sheet lined with parchment paper. Bake for 15-20 minutes, or until golden brown and the filling is heated through.
8. Let cool slightly before serving. You can drizzle with additional buffalo sauce for extra heat.

Tips

- To make your own buffalo sauce, combine melted butter, hot sauce, Worcestershire sauce, and a pinch of cayenne pepper.
- For a creamier filling, add a tablespoon of cream cheese to the buffalo chicken mixture.

Alex & Jamie
Blake

Nutritional Information (per serving)

Calories: 550, **Fat**: 25g,
Protein: 35g, **Carbs**: 50g

These air-fried calzones offer a twist on the classic calzone, filled with spicy buffalo chicken and your favorite toppings.

SERVES
4 - 6

PREP TIME
10 minutes

COOK TIME
10 - 12 minutes

SWEET NUTELLA AND BANANA PIZZA

Ingredients

- 1 store-bought pizza dough (12-14 inch round)
- ¼ cup Nutella
- 2 ripe bananas, sliced
- ¼ cup chopped hazelnuts (optional)
- 1 tablespoon powdered sugar (for dusting)

Instructions

1. Preheat your Breville Smart Air Fryer Oven Pro to the "Pizza" function according to the manufacturer's instructions. This will typically be around 480°F (249°C).
2. Unroll the pizza dough and place it on a baking sheet lined with parchment paper.
3. Spread Nutella evenly over the entire pizza dough, leaving a 1-inch border around the edge.
4. Arrange sliced bananas evenly over the Nutella layer.
5. Sprinkle chopped hazelnuts over the bananas (if using).
6. Place the baking sheet with the pizza directly on the oven rack (consult your Breville manual for specific placement instructions).
7. Bake for 10-12 minutes, or until the crust is golden brown and the bananas are softened. Keep an eye on the pizza during cooking, as times may vary depending on your Breville model.
8. Let cool slightly before slicing and serving. Dust with powdered sugar for an extra touch of sweetness.

Tips

- If your Nutella is too thick, microwave it for a few seconds to make it spreadable.
- For a richer flavor, drizzle the pizza with a touch of melted dark chocolate after baking.
- You can substitute chopped walnuts or pecans for the hazelnuts.
- Feel free to get creative with toppings! Add a sprinkle of cinnamon, a dollop of whipped cream, or a drizzle of caramel sauce for an extra decadent dessert pizza.

Nutritional Information (per serving)
Calories: 250, **Fat**: 5g, **Protein**: 8g, **Carbs**: 40g

A delicious and decadent dessert option

Alex & Jamie
Blake

SWEET ENDINGS
10 AIR-FRIED DELIGHTS FOR YOUR BREVILLE SMART AIR FRYER OVEN PRO

Indulge your sweet tooth with this collection of delectable air-fried desserts! From classic cookies to fruity crumbles, your Breville Smart Air Fryer Oven Pro transforms into a bakery haven. Get ready for warm, gooey treats with less fat and oil compared to traditional frying methods.

Alex & Jamie
Blake

SERVES	PREP TIME	COOK TIME
12 - 14 Cookies	10 minutes	10 - 12 minutes

AIR-FRIED GOOEY CHOCOLATE CHIP COOKIES

Ingredients

- 1 cup all-purpose flour
- ½ teaspoon baking soda
- ¼ teaspoon salt
- ½ cup unsalted butter, softened
- ½ cup brown sugar, packed
- ¼ cup granulated sugar
- 1 large egg
- 1 teaspoon pure vanilla extract
- 1 ½ cups semisweet chocolate chips

Instructions

1. Preheat your Breville Smart Air Fryer Oven Pro to 325°F (165°C) using the "Air Fry" function. Lightly grease a baking sheet or the air fryer basket with cooking spray.
2. In a medium bowl, whisk together flour, baking soda, and salt.
3. In a separate bowl, cream together softened butter and sugars until light and fluffy. Beat in the egg and vanilla extract until well combined.
4. Gradually add the dry ingredients to the wet ingredients, mixing until just combined. Fold in the chocolate chips.
5. Drop rounded tablespoons of dough onto the prepared baking sheet or air fryer basket, leaving space between them for spreading.
6. Air Fry for 10-12 minutes, or until the edges are golden brown and the centers are set but still slightly soft.
7. Let the cookies cool on the baking sheet for a few minutes before transferring them to a wire rack to cool completely.

Tips

- For chewier cookies, air fry for a minute or two less.
- You can substitute chopped nuts, peanut butter chips, or dried fruit for the chocolate chips.
- Leftover cookies can be stored in an airtight container at room temperature for up to 3 days.

Nutritional Information (per cookie)
Calories: 250, **Fat**: 12g,
Protein: 2g, **Carbs**: 30g

A delicious and decadent dessert option

Alex & Jamie
Blake

AIR-FRIED MINI CHEESECAKES

Ingredients

For the Crust:
- 1 ½ cups graham cracker crumbs
- 3 tablespoons melted butter

For the Filling:
- 8 ounces cream cheese, softened
- ¼ cup granulated sugar
- 1 large egg
- ½ teaspoon vanilla extract
- Pinch of salt

Instructions

1. Preheat your Breville Smart Air Fryer Oven Pro to 300°F (150°C) using the "Air Fry" function. Lightly grease a muffin tin.
2. In a small bowl, combine graham cracker crumbs and melted butter. Press the mixture evenly into the bottom of each muffin tin cup.
3. In a large bowl, beat together softened cream cheese and sugar until smooth and creamy. Beat in the egg, vanilla extract, and salt until well combined.
4. Divide the cheesecake filling evenly among the prepared muffin tin cups.
5. Air Fry for 15-20 minutes, or until the edges are set and the centers are slightly jiggly.
6. Let the cheesecakes cool completely in the muffin tin before carefully removing them. Chill for at least an hour before serving.

Tips

- Top your cheesecakes with fresh fruit, chocolate sauce, or whipped cream.
- For a richer flavor, use brown sugar instead of granulated sugar in the filling.
- Leftover cheesecakes can be stored in an airtight container in the refrigerator for up to 3 days.

Please note: Cooking times may vary depending on the size and thickness of your food items. It's recommended to check your food for doneness a few minutes before the suggested cooking time is complete.

Nutritional Information
(per cheesecake)
Calories: 280, **Fat**: 18g, **Protein**: 4g, **Carbs**: 20g

Whip up a creamy filling, spoon it into muffin cups, and air-fry for perfectly portioned, deliciously crispy-crust cheesecakes

Alex & Jamie Blake

| SERVES 4 - 6 | PREP TIME 15 minutes | COOK TIME 20 - 25 minutes |

AIR-FRIED SPICED APPLE CRUMBLE

Ingredients

- 4 medium apples (such as Granny Smith or Gala), peeled and sliced
- 2 tablespoons lemon juice
- ¼ cup granulated sugar
- ¼ teaspoon ground cinnamon
- ¼ teaspoon ground nutmeg
- Pinch of salt

For the Crumble Topping:
- ½ cup all-purpose flour
- ¼ cup rolled oats
- ¼ cup brown sugar, packed
- 3 tablespoons cold unsalted butter, cubed

Instructions

1. Preheat your Breville Smart Air Fryer Oven Pro to 350°F (175°C) using the "Air Fry" function. Lightly grease a baking dish or ramekins.
2. In a large bowl, toss apple slices with lemon juice, sugar, cinnamon, nutmeg, and salt.
3. In a separate bowl, combine flour, oats, and brown sugar. Using a pastry cutter or your fingertips, work the cold butter into the dry ingredients until it resembles coarse crumbs.
4. Transfer the apple mixture to the prepared baking dish or ramekins. Sprinkle the crumble topping evenly over the apples.
5. Air Fry for 20-25 minutes, or until the apples are tender and the crumble topping is golden brown.
6. Let the crumble cool slightly before serving. Enjoy warm with a scoop of vanilla ice cream (optional).

Tips

- You can add a handful of chopped nuts, such as pecans or walnuts, to the crumble topping for extra texture.
- For a deeper flavor, sprinkle a tablespoon of brown sugar over the apples before adding the crumble topping.
- Leftover crumble can be stored in an airtight container at room temperature for up to 2 days. Reheat in the air fryer for a few minutes to crisp up the topping.

Nutritional Information (per serving)

Calories: 220, **Fat**: 7g,
Protein: 1g, **Carbs**: 40g

Cinnamon-infused apples topped with a crunchy oat crumble get perfectly golden brown and crispy, for a healthy and satisfying treat

AIR-FRIED BANANA BREAD

Ingredients

- 2 ripe bananas, mashed
- ¼ cup unsalted butter, melted and cooled slightly
- ½ cup granulated sugar
- 1 large egg
- 1 teaspoon vanilla extract
- 1 ½ cups all-purpose flour
- 1 teaspoon baking powder
- ½ teaspoon baking soda
- ¼ teaspoon salt
- ½ cup chopped walnuts (optional)

Instructions

1. Preheat your Breville Smart Air Fryer Oven Pro to 350°F (175°C) using the "Air Fry" function. Grease a loaf pan.
2. In a large bowl, mash the bananas until smooth. Stir in the melted butter, sugar, egg, and vanilla extract until well combined.
3. In a separate bowl, whisk together flour, baking powder, baking soda, and salt.
4. Gradually add the dry ingredients to the wet ingredients, mixing until just combined. Be careful not to overmix. Fold in the chopped walnuts (if using).
5. Pour the batter into the prepared loaf pan.
6. Air Fry for 40-45 minutes, or until a toothpick inserted into the center comes out clean.
7. Let the banana bread cool in the loaf pan for a few minutes before transferring it to a wire rack to cool completely.

Tips

- You can substitute other chopped nuts, such as pecans or almonds, for the walnuts.
- For a chocolate chip twist, add ½ cup of semisweet chocolate chips to the batter.
- Leftover banana bread can be stored in an airtight container at room temperature for up to 3 days or frozen for up to 3 months.

Nutritional Information (per slice)

Calories: 200, **Fat**: 7g, **Protein**: 2g, **Carbs**: 30g

This moist and flavorful banana bread is perfect for a quick and satisfying breakfast or snack.

SERVES
4 - 6

PREP TIME
15 minutes

COOK TIME
25 - 30 minutes

AIR-FRIED PINEAPPLE UPSIDE-DOWN CAKE

Ingredients

- 3 tablespoons unsalted butter
- ¼ cup packed brown sugar
- 1 can (15 oz) sliced pineapple rings, drained (reserve maraschino cherries from the can)
- ½ cup maraschino cherries, halved
- ½ cup all-purpose flour
- ½ teaspoon baking powder
- ¼ teaspoon baking soda
- ¼ teaspoon salt
- ¼ cup granulated sugar
- 1 large egg
- 2 tablespoons milk
- 1 teaspoon vanilla extract

Instructions

1. Preheat your Breville Smart Air Fryer Oven Pro to 325°F (165°C) using the "Air Fry" function. Lightly grease a small oven-safe dish or ramekins.
2. In a small saucepan, melt butter over medium heat. Add brown sugar and stir constantly until melted and bubbly. Remove from heat and pour the caramel mixture into the prepared dish, coating the bottom evenly.
3. Arrange pineapple rings on top of the caramel, leaving a small space in the center. Place a cherry half in the center of each pineapple ring.
4. In a medium bowl, whisk together flour, baking powder, baking soda, and salt.
5. In a separate bowl, whisk together granulated sugar, egg, milk, and vanilla extract until well combined.
6. Gently fold the wet ingredients into the dry ingredients until just combined. Be careful not to overmix.
7. Pour the cake batter over the pineapple rings in the prepared dish, spreading it evenly.
8. Air Fry for 25-30 minutes, or until a toothpick inserted into the center comes out clean.
9. Let the cake cool slightly in the dish before inverting it onto a plate. Serve warm with a scoop of vanilla ice cream (optional).

Tips

- You can use fresh pineapple chunks instead of canned pineapple rings. However, make sure to pat them dry to prevent excess moisture.
- For a richer flavor, substitute melted butter with melted coconut oil in the caramel mixture.

Nutritional Information (per serving)

Calories: 280, **Fat**: 10g, **Protein**: 2g, **Carbs**: 40g

This classic dessert gets a healthy makeover with air-frying! Enjoy the caramelized sweetness of pineapple and cherries nestled in a moist cake.

AIR-FRIED MINI PEACH MELBAS

Ingredients

- 2 ripe peaches, halved and pitted
- 1 tablespoon honey
- ¼ teaspoon ground cinnamon
- ½ cup fresh raspberries
- 1 tablespoon powdered sugar
- 1 cup whipping cream
- 1 teaspoon vanilla extract

Instructions

1. Preheat your Breville Smart Air Fryer Oven Pro to 375°F (190°C) using the "Air Fry" function.
2. In a small bowl, combine honey and cinnamon. Brush the cut side of the peach halves with the honey mixture.
3. Place the peach halves, cut side down, in the air fryer basket.
4. Air Fry for 10-12 minutes, or until the peaches are softened and slightly caramelized.
5. Meanwhile, in a small blender or food processor, puree the raspberries with powdered sugar until smooth. Strain the coulis to remove any seeds.
6. In a separate bowl, whip the whipping cream with vanilla extract until soft peaks form.
7. To assemble the melbas, place an air-fried peach half on a plate. Spoon some raspberry coulis over the peach, and top it with a dollop of whipped cream.

Tips

- You can substitute other stone fruits, such as nectarines or plums, for the peaches.
- For a richer coulis, add a tablespoon of red wine to the raspberries before blending.
- Leftover coulis can be stored in an airtight container in the refrigerator for up to 3 days.

Nutritional Information
(per serving)

Calories: 250, **Fat**: 10g,
Protein: 2g, **Carbs**: 35g

These elegant individual desserts feature air-fried peaches topped with a sweet raspberry coulis and a dollop of whipped cream.

SERVES	PREP TIME	COOK TIME
4	5 minutes	4 - 5 minutes

AIR-FRIED PEANUT BUTTER AND BANANA QUESADILLAS

Ingredients

- 2 large tortillas
- 2 tablespoons creamy peanut butter
- 1 ripe banana, sliced
- ¼ cup chopped dark chocolate (optional)
- Pinch of ground cinnamon

Instructions

1. Preheat your Breville Smart Air Fryer Oven Pro to 350°F (175°C) using the "Air Fry" function.
2. Spread a tablespoon of peanut butter on one half of each tortilla.
3. Top the peanut butter with sliced banana.
4. If using, sprinkle chopped dark chocolate over the bananas.
5. Fold the tortillas in half, enclosing the filling.
6. Lightly brush the outside of the quesadillas with melted butter or cooking spray (optional) for extra crispiness.
7. Place the quesadillas in the air fryer basket, leaving space between them.
8. Air Fry for 4-5 minutes per side, or until golden brown and crispy.
9. Let the quesadillas cool slightly before slicing and serving. Dust with a pinch of ground cinnamon for an extra flavor boost (optional).

Tips

- You can substitute almond butter for peanut butter.
- For a more decadent treat, add a drizzle of honey or maple syrup over the quesadillas before serving.
- Leftover quesadillas can be stored in an airtight container in the refrigerator for up to 2 days. Reheat in the air fryer for a few minutes to crisp them back up.

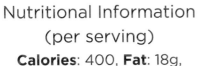

Nutritional Information
(per serving)
Calories: 400, **Fat**: 18g,
Protein: 8g, **Carbs**: 50g

These warm and gooey quesadillas are a fun twist on a classic dessert, perfect for satisfying a sweet tooth with a touch of protein.

SERVES	PREP TIME	COOK TIME
10 - 12 fritters	5 minutes	4 - 5 minutes

AIR-FRIED MINI APPLE FRITTERS

Ingredients

- 1 cup all-purpose flour
- 2 tablespoons granulated sugar
- 1 teaspoon baking powder
- ½ teaspoon ground cinnamon
- ¼ teaspoon salt
- ½ cup milk
- 1 large egg
- 1 teaspoon vanilla extract
- 1 apple, peeled and diced
- Vegetable oil for frying (optional)

Instructions

1. Preheat your Breville Smart Air Fryer Oven Pro to 375°F (190°C) using the "Air Fry" function. Lightly grease the air fryer basket or coat it with a thin layer of cooking spray.
2. In a medium bowl, whisk together flour, sugar, baking powder, cinnamon, and salt.
3. In a separate bowl, whisk together milk, egg, and vanilla extract until well combined.
4. Add the wet ingredients to the dry ingredients and stir until just combined. Be careful not to overmix. Fold in the diced apples.
5. The batter should be thick and slightly sticky. If it's too dry, add a tablespoon or two of milk.
6. You can use a spoon or a cookie scoop to portion the batter into the prepared air fryer basket, leaving space between them. Alternatively, for a deeper golden brown color, you can shallow fry the fritters in a pan with about 1/4 inch of hot vegetable oil.
7. Air Fry for 5-7 minutes per side, or until golden brown and cooked through. If shallow frying, cook for 2-3 minutes per side.
8. Drain the fritters on paper towels to remove excess oil.
9. Serve the fritters warm, dusted with powdered sugar (optional).

Tips

- You can substitute other fruits, such as pears or peaches, for the apples.
- For a richer flavor, add a teaspoon of ground nutmeg to the dry ingredients.

Nutritional Information
(per serving)
Calories: 400, **Fat**: 18g,
Protein: 8g, **Carbs**: 50g

These fluffy apple fritters are a delicious way to enjoy apples with a crispy, air-fried coating.

| SERVES 4 - 6 | PREP TIME 15 minutes | COOK TIME 5 - 7 minutes |

CHURROS WITH CHOCOLATE DIPPING SAUCE

Ingredients

For the Churros:
- 1 cup all-purpose flour
- ½ teaspoon salt
- 1 cup water
- 2 tablespoons unsalted butter
- 1 large egg
- Vegetable oil for frying (optional)

For the Chocolate Dipping Sauce:
- ¾ cup semisweet chocolate chips
- ¾ cup heavy cream
- 1 teaspoon vanilla extract

Instructions

1. Preheat your Breville Smart Air Fryer Oven Pro to 400°F (200°C) using the "Air Fry" function. Lightly grease the air fryer basket or coat it with a thin layer of cooking spray.
2. In a medium saucepan, combine water and butter. Bring to a boil over medium heat.
3. Remove the pan from heat and stir in the flour and salt all at once. Stir vigorously until a dough ball forms.
4. Transfer the dough to a mixing bowl and let it cool slightly for about 5 minutes.
5. In a separate bowl, beat the egg until well combined. Add the egg to the dough a little at a time, beating well after each addition until the dough becomes smooth and pipeable.
6. Transfer the dough to a piping bag fitted with a star tip.
7. You can use a spoon or pipe the dough into long, thin strips directly into the prepared air fryer basket, leaving space between them. Alternatively, for a deeper golden brown color, you can shallow fry the churros in a pan with about 1/4 inch of hot vegetable oil.
8. Air Fry for 5-7 minutes per side, or until golden brown and crispy. If shallow frying, cook for 1-2 minutes per side.
9. Drain the churros on paper towels to remove excess oil.

For the Chocolate Dipping Sauce:

1. In a small saucepan, heat heavy cream over medium heat until simmering. Do not let it boil.
2. Remove the pan from heat and add chocolate chips. Let it sit for 1 minute, then stir until smooth and melted.
3. Stir in vanilla extract.

Nutritional Information
(per churro)
Calories: 150, **Fat**: 7g,
Protein: 2g, **Carbs**: 20g

These light and crispy churros are a fun and easy air-fried treat, perfect for dipping in a rich chocolate sauce

SERVES 12 - 14	PREP TIME 15 minutes	COOK TIME 5 - 7 minutes

AIR-FRIED MINI DOUGHNUTS

Ingredients

- 1 ½ cups all-purpose flour
- ¼ cup granulated sugar
- 2 teaspoons baking powder
- ½ teaspoon salt
- ½ cup milk
- 1 large egg
- 2 tablespoons unsalted butter, melted and cooled slightly
- 1 teaspoon vanilla extract

- Vegetable oil for greasing (optional)

For Glazing (Optional):
- ½ cup powdered sugar
- 2-3 tablespoons milk
- Food coloring (optional)

Instructions

1. Preheat your Breville Smart Air Fryer Oven Pro to 350°F (175°C) using the "Air Fry" function. Lightly grease a doughnut mold or a baking sheet with vegetable oil (optional).
2. In a medium bowl, whisk together flour, sugar, baking powder, and salt.
3. In a separate bowl, whisk together milk, egg, melted butter, and vanilla extract until well combined.
4. Add the wet ingredients to the dry ingredients and stir until just combined. Be careful not to overmix, as this can make the doughnuts tough.
5. Transfer the batter to a piping bag fitted with a star tip (or a ziplock bag with a corner snipped off).
6. Pipe the batter into the prepared doughnut mold, filling each cavity about ¾ full. Alternatively, pipe small rounds of dough onto the baking sheet, leaving space between them for spreading.
7. Air Fry for 5-7 minutes, or until the doughnuts are golden brown and cooked through. You can check for doneness by inserting a toothpick into the center of a doughnut; it should come out clean.
8. Let the doughnuts cool slightly in the mold or on the baking sheet for a few minutes before transferring them to a wire rack to cool completely.
9. For Glazing (Optional):
10. In a small bowl, whisk together powdered sugar and milk until you have a smooth and thick glaze. You can adjust the consistency of the glaze by adding more milk for a thinner glaze or more powdered sugar for a thicker glaze.
11. If desired, add a few drops of food coloring to the glaze for a fun touch.
12. Once the doughnuts are cool, dip them one by one into the glaze, letting any excess drip off before placing them back on the wire rack to set.

Nutritional Information (per doughnut)
Calories: 150, **Fat**: 5g, **Protein**: 2g, **Carbs**: 25g

These light and fluffy mini doughnuts are a healthier take on the classic dessert. Enjoy them glazed with your favorite flavors, or simply plain!

Conquering the Kitchen: Essential Conversion Charts & Equivalents

In the culinary world, precision plays a vital role. The perfect balance of ingredients is what separates a delightful dish from a culinary disaster. But recipe measurements can sometimes feel like a foreign language, with cups, ounces, grams, and milliliters swirling in a confusing dance. Fear not, fellow food enthusiasts! This chapter equips you with essential conversion charts and equivalents, transforming you into a measurement maestro in the kitchen.

Conversion Charts: Your Culinary Compass

Imagine a world where you can effortlessly convert between cups of flour and grams of sugar, or seamlessly switch between Fahrenheit and Celsius for baking temperatures. This chapter equips you with three key conversion charts to navigate recipe measurements with confidence:

- Volume Conversions: This chart tackles the common battle between cups and milliliters (ml), ounces (oz), and fluid ounces (fl oz). It allows you to convert wet and dry ingredients with ease, ensuring you never end up with a soup instead of a cake batter.

Measurement	Equivalent in Milliliters (ml)	Equivalent in Ounces (oz)	Equivalent in Fluid Ounces (fl oz)
1 cup	240 ml	8 oz	8 fl oz
½ cup	120 ml	4 oz	4 fl oz
¼ cup	60 ml	2 oz	2 fl oz
1 tablespoon (Tbsp)	15 ml	½ oz	½ fl oz
1 teaspoon (tsp)	5 ml	¼ oz	¼ fl oz

- Weight Conversions: This chart focuses on grams (g) and ounces (oz), allowing you to precisely measure dry ingredients like flour, sugar, and spices. No more overflowing measuring spoons or under-filled baking pans!

Measurement	Equivalent in Grams (g)	Equivalent in Ounces (oz)
1 pound (lb)	454 g	16 oz
½ pound (lb)	227 g	8 oz
¼ pound (lb)	113 g	4 oz
1 cup all-purpose flour	120 g	4.2 oz
1 cup granulated sugar	200 g	7.1 oz
1 cup brown sugar, packed	220 g	7.8 oz

- Temperature Conversions: This chart bridges the gap between Fahrenheit (°F) and Celsius (°C), crucial for baking and cooking where temperature control is essential. No more scrambling to convert oven temperatures or wondering if the water is hot enough for boiling pasta.

Temperature (°F)	Equivalent in Celsius (°C)
350 °F	175 °C
375 °F	190 °C
400 °F	200 °C
425 °F	220 °C
450 °F	230 °C

Maintaining Your Breville Smart Air Fryer Oven Pro: A Recipe for Longevity

Your Breville Smart Air Fryer Oven Pro is an investment in healthy and convenient cooking. Just like any prized possession, proper cleaning and maintenance are essential to ensure its longevity and optimal performance. This chapter equips you with easy-to-follow instructions for cleaning the various components of your Air Fryer Oven, keeping it sparkling clean and ready for culinary adventures.

Gather Your Cleaning Arsenal

Before you embark on your cleaning quest, assemble your cleaning supplies:
1. Warm, soapy water
2. Soft sponge or dishcloth
3. Non-abrasive cleaning pad (optional)
4. Microfiber cloth
5. Baking soda (optional)
6. White vinegar (optional)

Important Reminders

1. Always unplug your Breville Smart Air Fryer Oven Pro and allow it to cool completely before cleaning.
2. Never immerse the appliance or cord in water.
3. Do not use harsh chemicals, abrasive cleaners, or scouring pads, as they can damage the non-stick coating.

Cleaning the Exterior

- Wipe down the exterior of the appliance with a damp microfiber cloth.
- For stubborn grease stains, dampen the cloth with warm, soapy water and wipe clean. Dry thoroughly with a clean microfiber cloth.

Cleaning the Interior

- Remove the air fryer basket and crumb tray.
- Wash the basket and crumb tray with warm, soapy water. You can use a soft sponge or dishcloth for gentle scrubbing. If needed, a non-abrasive cleaning pad can be used for stubborn grease stains.
- Rinse the basket and crumb tray thoroughly and pat them dry with a clean cloth.
- Wipe down the interior walls of the oven with a damp microfiber cloth. For stuck-on food particles, you can create a paste with baking soda and water. Apply the paste to the affected area, let it sit for a few minutes, and then wipe clean with a damp cloth.
- Clean the door window with a damp microfiber cloth or a solution of white vinegar and water (½ cup water to 1 tablespoon white vinegar)

Deep Cleaning (Optional)

For a deeper clean every few months, you can soak the air fryer basket and crumb tray in warm, soapy water for about 30 minutes to loosen stubborn grease and food residue.

Cleaning the Heating Element (Optional)

While the heating element is self-cleaning during operation, you can occasionally wipe it down with a damp cloth to remove any visible food particles.

Drying is Key

Ensure all components are completely dry before reassembling your Breville Smart Air Fryer Oven Pro. Leaving any moisture can lead to rust or mold growth.

Storing Your Breville Smart Air Fryer Oven Pro

When not in use, store your Breville Smart Air Fryer Oven Pro in a cool, dry place. If storing for an extended period, you can place a baking sheet or parchment paper on the bottom rack to prevent dust accumulation within the oven cavity.

By following these simple cleaning and maintenance tips, you can ensure your Breville Smart Air Fryer Oven Pro remains a reliable and functional kitchen companion for years to come. A little care goes a long way in preserving the performance and longevity of your appliance, allowing you to continue creating delicious and healthy air-fried meals for countless culinary adventures. So, grab your cleaning supplies, and keep your air fryer sparkling clean for a lifetime of crispy perfection!

Conclusion

Congratulations, air-frying aficionados! You've reached the final chapter of this culinary odyssey, armed with the knowledge and inspiration to conquer the kitchen with your Breville Smart Air Fryer Oven Pro. This book has been your faithful companion, guiding you through the wonders of air-frying, from unlocking its various functions to mastering essential techniques and discovering a treasure trove of delicious recipes.

But consider this merely the first chapter in your air-frying saga. The true magic lies in the boundless potential that awaits.

A Feast for the Future

This comprehensive guide has equipped you with a diverse arsenal of recipes, catering to every craving, dietary preference, and occasion. From breakfast delights to satisfying snacks, succulent meats to delightful vegetarian options, and sweet treats to quick weeknight meals, you now possess the culinary prowess to whip up a feast for any occasion.

Beyond the Recipe Realm

Remember, these recipes are just the launching pad for your culinary creativity. Don't be afraid to experiment! Substitute ingredients, explore new flavor combinations, and unleash your inner chef to create signature air-fried dishes that tantalize your taste buds and become conversation starters at every gathering.

A Toast to Healthier Indulgence

Let's not forget the air-frying revolution's core principle: healthier indulgence. This innovative appliance allows you to enjoy your favorite foods with significantly less fat and fewer calories compared to traditional frying methods. So, raise a metaphorical glass (or maybe a steaming basket of perfectly crisped vegetables) to a future filled with delicious and guilt-free meals.

A Final Note

As you embark on your air-frying adventures, remember to revisit the valuable resources in this book.

The Final Toast

May your Breville Smart Air Fryer Oven Pro continue to be your loyal sidekick in the kitchen, helping you create countless culinary memories and air-fried masterpieces for years to come. So, here's to a lifetime of delicious exploration, healthier indulgences, and a world of air-frying possibilities waiting to be devoured.

Happy Air-Frying!